TO AH'LIVIA RICHARDSON

CONGRATULATIONS ON

YOUR GRADUATION TO

1ST GRADE

JULY 8, 2018

ALLEN CHAPEL CME CHURCH

Ah'Livia

Richardson

With 61 Stories from the
International Children's Bible

PUBLISHING COMPANY LLC

ATLANTA, GEORGIA USA

Children of Color
Storybook
BIBLE

ISBN: 978-0-9846480-0-9

Contents

Stories from the Old Testament

Stories from the New Testament

Welcome to the International Children's Bible

The International Children's Bible is an edition of the New Century Version, which is a translation of God's Word from the original Hebrew and Greek languages. This is the first translation of the Holy Scriptures prepared especially for children. Until now, children have had to learn God's truths from adult-language Bibles or books based on them. Many words and concepts readily understood by adults may leave children mystified or even with false impressions.

Yet God intended for everyone to be able to understand his Word. Earliest Scriptures were in Hebrew, ideally suited for a barely literate society because of its economy of words, acrostic literary form, and poetic parallelism. The New Testament was first written in the simple Greek of everyday life, not in the Latin of Roman courts or the classical Greek of the academies. Even Jesus, the Master Teacher, taught spiritual principles by comparing them to such familiar terms as pearls, seeds, rocks, trees, and sheep. It is for this same purpose of making the Scriptures intelligible, even to children, that this translation was created.

The International Children's Bible is faithful to the manuscripts in the original languages, yet it is simple enough for children to read and understand for themselves. Special care has been taken in rendering passages that refer to ancient customs, or use language with variable connotations or figures of speech. Some passages are further explained by footnotes, indicated in the text by a raised letter *n*.

We acknowledge the infallibility of God's word and our own human frailty. We pray that God has worked through us as his vessels, and it is to his glory that this Bible is given.

To Parents

Love the Lord your God with all your heart, soul
and strength. Always remember these commands I
give you today. Teach them to your children. Talk
about them when you sit at home and walk along
the road. Talk about them when you lie down and
when you get up.

Deuteronomy 6:5–7

Using Children of Color Storybook Bible

This marvelous instruction from God's Word is a guideline for all
parents in leading their children to the Lord. We are told to first *love*
the Lord, then memorize his Word, his laws. Once we have our own relationship with God, he will lead us in talking about him and his Word
to our children.

We hope this book will help. Its design is two-fold: 1) for parents to
read to their younger children, sharing with them the marvelous adven-
tures and lessons from the Bible; and 2) for older children to read for
themselves, exploring the world of the Bible and the people who gave
birth to our faith. The main text of the stories is from the International
Children's Bible, which is easy for children to understand, both as it is
read to them and as they learn to read for themselves. Occasionally,
some transitional paragraphs have been provided in order to move children from one story to another. These are printed in a slightly lighter
typeface, so they can be distinguished from the actual Bible text, which
is darker.

Most parents hope that their children will come to love the Lord. We
can help by providing them with the stories they love and understand,
explaining to them how much God loves each and every one of them,
and, most importantly, by being a spiritual model for them.

A Word from Children of Color

Children of Color Publishing has chosen to develop Bible products that help to build the self-esteem of young people of African descent and has thoughtfully and prayerfully designed the *Children of Color Storybook Bible* for your child of color.

Young people need to understand that their heritage and history began long before civil rights and slavery and that the events and stories in the Bible are a part of that heritage—they took place on the very continent, Africa, especially northeastern Africa, where their ancestors lived and died. Knowing this can help children gain the confidence and courage to overcome the many obstacles they will encounter growing up in the world today.

Children are fearfully and wonderfully made. They should know that they are made in the image of God and that the Bible is talking about them when they read that believers can be victorious through Christ (Romans 8:37). They will profit greatly from being personally convinced that Christ can give them the strength to face anything (Philippians 3:14), and—most importantly—that Christ is their personal Savior. Presenting the Bible in a way to which African-American children and other minorities can relate makes achieving the goal much easier.

Give your children an early start: Read this beautiful Bible with your children daily. Teach them the principles that are in each story. Instill in them at an early age that the Bible is God's Word and our foundation for living. The best way to show your kids how to be a part of God's family, however, is to live your relationship with the Lord openly. Let them see you reading your own Bible and enjoying your own place in God's kingdom.

Children of Color
Storybook
BIBLE

The Story of Creation

In the beginning the earth was dark and empty. There was nothing to see—no people, no animals, and no trees. Not a living thing existed. Then God said, "Let there be light!" And there was light. God saw that the light was good. So he divided

the light from the darkness. God named the light "day" and the darkness "night." Evening passed, and morning came. This was the first day that the Lord made.

On the second day God created the sky. That was the second day that the Lord made.

On the third day God said, "Let the water under the sky be gathered together so the dry land will appear." And it happened. God named the dry land "earth." He named the water that was gathered together "seas." He also commanded that the plants, trees, fruit and grain grow. Beautiful greenery filled the earth. **God saw that all this was good.** That was the third day that the Lord made.

On the fourth day God said, "Let there be lights in the sky to separate day from night. These lights will be used for signs, seasons, days and years." God also made two powerful lights, the brighter one, called the sun, to rule the day and the other, called the moon, to rule the night. Then God made the

stars and put them and the rest of the lights in the sky to shine on the earth. **God saw that all these things were good.** That was the fourth day that the Lord made.

On the fifth day God created the living creatures of the sea and birds to fly above the earth. **God blessed them and said, "Have many young ones and grow in number. Fill the water of the seas, and let the birds grow in number on the earth."** That was the fifth day that the Lord made.

On the sixth day God created all kinds of tame and wild animals. This was the day he also created the people to be like himself. They would rule the fish, birds and other living creatures. **God looked at everything he had made, and it was very good.** That was the sixth day that the Lord made.

By the seventh day God finished the work he had been
doing. So on the seventh day he rested from all his work. God

blessed the seventh day and made it a holy day. God was very pleased with all he had done.

from **Genesis 1:1—2:3**

Adam and Eve

Then the Lord God took dust from the ground and formed man from it. The Lord breathed the breath of life into the man's nose. And the man became a living person. The first man was called Adam. Then the Lord God planted a garden in the East, in a place called Eden. The Lord God put the man in the garden of Eden to care for it and work it. The garden of Eden was a beautiful

place. The Lord God caused every beautiful tree and every tree that was good for food to grow out of the ground. In the middle of the garden, God put the tree that gives life. And he put there the tree that gives the knowledge of good and evil.

God told Adam, "You may eat the fruit from any tree in the garden. But you must not eat the fruit from the tree which gives the knowledge of good and evil. If you ever eat fruit from that tree, you will die!"

God decided it was not good for man to live alone. God put   7

Adam in a deep sleep and removed one of his ribs. The **Lord God** used the rib from the man to make a woman. Her name was Eve. Eve was the first woman. When Adam woke up, he was excited to see another person.

Adam and Eve lived happily in the Garden of Eden, obeying God's rules and enjoying the beautiful plants and animals.

Now the snake was the most clever of all the wild animals the Lord God had made. One day the snake spoke to the woman. He said, "Did God really say that you must not eat fruit from any tree in the garden?"

The woman answered the snake, "We may eat fruit from the trees in the garden. But God told us, 'You must not eat fruit from the tree that is in the middle of the garden. You must not even touch it, or you will die.' "

But the snake said to the woman, "You will not die. God knows that if you eat the fruit from that tree, you will learn about good and evil. Then you will be like God!"

Eve wanted the wisdom that the tree would give her. So she took a piece of fruit from the tree and bit it! She also gave some of the fruit to her husband, and he ate it.

Then, it was as if the man's and the woman's eyes were opened. They realized they had disobeyed God. They became frightened and tried to hide from God.

Later, the Lord called out to Adam. "Where are you? Why are you hiding yourself from me? Did you eat fruit from that tree?"

Adam answered, "You gave this woman to me. She gave me fruit from the tree. So I ate it."

God asked Eve, "What have you done?"

She answered, "The snake tricked me. So I ate the fruit." So the Lord cursed the snake to crawl on his stomach and eat dirt. Then he cursed Eve to suffer terribly during childbirth.

To Adam the Lord said, "You listened to what your wife said. And you ate fruit from the tree that I commanded you not to eat from. So, I will put a curse on the ground. You will have to work very hard for food. In pain you will eat its food all the days of your life. The ground will produce thorns and weeds for you. And you will eat the plants of the field. You will sweat and work hard for your food. Later you will return to the ground. This is because you were taken from the ground. You are dust. And when you die, you will return to the dust."

So the Lord God forced the man out of the garden of Eden. He had to work the ground he was taken from.

from Genesis 2:7—3:23

Cain
and Abel

After being thrown out of the Garden of Eden, Adam and Eve had two sons. Their names were Cain and Abel. **Abel took** care of sheep. Cain became a farmer.

Later, Cain brought a gift to God. He brought some food

from the ground. Abel brought the best parts of his best sheep. The Lord accepted Abel and his gift. But God did not accept Cain and his gift. Cain became very angry and looked unhappy.

The Lord asked Cain, "Why are you angry? Why do you look so unhappy? If you do good, I will accept you. But if you do not do good, sin is ready to attack you. Sin wants you. But you must rule over it."

Cain said to his brother Abel, "Let's go out in the field." So   *11*

Cain and Abel went into the field. Then Cain attacked his brother Abel and killed him.

Later, the Lord said to Cain, "Where is your brother Abel?"

Cain answered, "I don't know. Is it my job to take care of my brother?

Then the Lord said, "What have you done? Your brother's blood is on the ground. That blood is like a voice that tells me what happened. And now you will be cursed in your work with the ground. It is the same ground where your brother's blood fell. Your hands killed him. You will work the ground. But it will not  grow good crops for you anymore. You will wander around on the earth."

Then Cain said to the Lord, "This punishment is more than I can stand! Look! You have forced me to stop working the ground. And now I must hide from you. I will wander around on the earth. And anyone who meets me can kill me."

Then the Lord said to Cain, "No! If anyone kills you, I will punish that person seven times more." Then the Lord put a mark on Cain. It was a warning to anyone who met him not to kill him.

Then Cain went away from the Lord. Cain lived in the land of Nod,[n] east of Eden.

from Genesis 4:2–16

Noah

There were many evil people on the earth, and God was not pleased with them. So the Lord said, "I will destroy all human beings that I made on the earth. And I will destroy every animal and everything that crawls on the earth. I will also destroy the birds of the air. This is because I am sorry that I have made them."

However, there was one man that pleased God. His name

was Noah. He was the most innocent man of his time. He walked with God. God told Noah that he was planning to destroy the whole world and all of its people. He instructed Noah to build a boat that was three stories high and put a door on one side. He promised Noah that he, his wife, his sons and their wives would be kept safe in the boat, or ark as this boat is sometimes called.

Then the Lord said to Noah, "I have seen that you are the best man among the people of this time. So you and your family go into the boat. Take two of every animal. One male and one fe- **15** male. This will allow all these animals to continue living on the earth after the flood. Seven days from now I will send rain on the earth. It will rain 40 days and 40 nights. I will destroy from the earth every living thing that I made."

Noah did exactly as God told him. Noah, his family and the animals got in the ark just as God said.

The rain fell on the earth for 40 days and 40 nights. Water even came up out of the earth. The water continued to rise, and the boat floated on the water above the earth. The water rose so much that even the highest mountains under the sky were covered by it.

So God destroyed from the earth every living thing that was on the land. This was every man, animal, crawling thing and bird of the sky. All that was left was Noah and what was with him in the boat. They had trusted and obeyed God.

God was again pleased. He blessed Noah and his family for their obedience. God promised never to destroy the earth with a flood again. God placed a rainbow of magnificent colors in the sky as a sign of his promise.

God said to Noah and his sons:

"I am putting my rainbow in the clouds. It is the sign of the agreement between me and the earth. When I bring clouds over the earth, a rainbow appears in the clouds. Then I will remember my agreement. It is between me and you and every living thing. Floodwaters will never again destroy all life on the earth. When the rainbow appears in the clouds, I will see it. Then I will remember the agreement that continues forever. It is between me and every living thing on the earth."

So God said to Noah, "That rainbow is a sign. It is the sign of the agreement that I made with all living things on earth."

from Genesis 6:5—9:17

Nimrod and the Descendants of Ham

A fter the flood, Noah and his sons, Shem, Ham and Japheth, came out of the boat. These three men were Noah's sons. And all the people on earth came from these three sons. Ham was the father of Cush (Ethiopia), Mizraim (Egypt), Put and

Canaan, and they were the ancestors of the kingdoms named after them.

All these people were the sons of Ham. All these families had their own languages, their own lands and their own nations. African-American people and other people of color, such as Asians and Indians, are descendants of Ham.

One of Ham's descendants, Cush, was the father of many sons, and he also had a descendant named Nimrod. Nimrod became a very powerful man on earth. He was a great hunter before the Lord. That is why people say someone is "like Nimrod, a great hunter before the Lord." At first Nimrod's kingdom covered Babylon, Erech, Akkad and Calneh in the land of Babylonia. From there he went to Assyria. There he built the cities of Nineveh, Rehoboth Ir and Calah. He also built Resen, the great city between Nineveh and Calah.

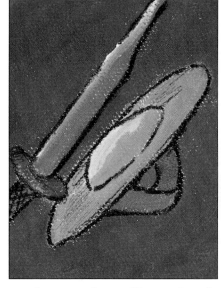

Nimrod was the world's first mighty warrior, and he built many great cities. "Rehoboth Ir" was Hebrew for "broad places of the city" and may have been a suburb of Nineveh. Calah was located between two great rivers. Later, it was the military headquarters of the Assyrians, and they launched some of their greatest battles from there. "Resen" means "fountainhead" and was part of a cluster of cities that was more than 60 miles across!

Nimrod was a great warrior and a mighty hunter, but he was also a terrific king! Nimrod built a great kingdom in Assyria, which became known as "the land of Nimrod."

He also built an empire in the land of Shinar. Nimrod built the great city of Babel, which is where all the languages in the world came from. His other cities included Erech, Calneh and Akkad, which was the capital of an empire that ruled the Middle East for almost 300 years! In fact, Nimrod brought to the Middle East a new type of government that improved the way people lived, worked and spent their money.

His reign over his kingdoms was so successful that many of

the empires that ruled part of the Middle East for more than 2,000 years could be traced to the mighty warrior, Nimrod.

from **Genesis 9:19; 10:6–12**

Sodom and Gomorrah

Then the Lord said to Abraham, "I have heard many things against the people of Sodom and Gomorrah. They are very evil. So I will go down and see if they are as bad as I have heard."

Abraham asked, "Lord, do you plan to destroy the good persons along with the evil persons? What if there are 50 good people

in that city? Will you still destroy it? Surely you will save the city for the 50 good people living there. Surely you will not destroy the good people along with the evil people. Then the good people and the evil people would be treated the same. You are the judge of all the earth. Won't you do what is right?"

Then the Lord said, "If I find 50 good people in the city of Sodom, I will save the whole city because of them."

Then Abraham said, "I am only dust and ashes. Yet I have

23

been brave to speak to the Lord. What if there are only 45 good people in the city? Will you destroy the whole city for the lack of 5 good people?"

The Lord said, "If I find 45 good people there, I will not destroy the city."

Again Abraham said to the Lord, "If you find only 40 good people there, will you destroy the city?"

The Lord said, "If I find 40 good people, I will not destroy the city."

Then Abraham said, "Lord, please don't be angry with me. Let me ask you this. If you find only 30 good people in the city, will you destroy it?"

The Lord said, "If I find 30 good people there, I will not destroy the city."

Then Abraham said, "I have been brave to speak to the Lord. But what if there are only 20 good people in the city?"

The Lord answered, "If I find 20 good people there, I will not destroy the city."

Then Abraham said, "Lord, please don't be angry with me. Let me bother you this one last time. What if you find 10 good people there?"

The Lord said, "If I find 10 good people there, I will not destroy it."

Lot was the nephew of Abraham, and he lived in Sodom with his family. Lot was one of the very few "good people" who lived in Sodom. Two angels appeared to Lot and told him to leave

Sodom with his family and not to look back at the destruction of the city.

After Lot and his family ran from the city, the Lord sent a rain of burning sulfur down from the sky on Sodom and Gomorrah. So the Lord destroyed those cities. He also destroyed the whole Jordan Valley, everyone living in the cities and even all the plants.

In disobedience, Lot's wife stopped to look back at the burning cities. Instantly, she was turned into a block of salt. But the Lord remembered what Abraham had asked. So God saved Lot's life.

from **Genesis 18:20—19:29**

Abraham and Isaac

Abraham and Sarah were very old, and Sarah was well past the age for having children. Even so, the Lord promised that they would have a son, and the Lord did bless them with a fine son. His name was Isaac.

After these things God tested Abraham's faith. Then God said, "Take your only son, Isaac, the son you love. Go to the land of Moriah. There kill him and offer him as a whole burnt offering. Do this on one of the mountains there. I will tell you which one."

Early in the morning Abraham got up and saddled his donkey. He cut the wood for the sacrifice. Abraham, Isaac, a donkey and two servants set out for the place where God had instructed him to go.

On the third day Abraham looked up and saw the place in the distance. He said to his servants, "Stay here with the donkey. My son and I will go over there and worship. Then we will come back to you."

Abraham took the wood for the sacrifice and gave it to his son to carry. Abraham took the knife and the fire. So Abraham and his son went on together.

Isaac said, "We have the fire and the wood. But where is the lamb we will burn as a sacrifice?"

Abraham answered, "God will give us the lamb for the sacrifice, my son."

The two reached the place where the Lord had told Abraham to go. There, Abraham built an altar. He laid the wood on it. Then he tied up his son Isaac. And he laid Isaac on the wood on the altar. Then Abraham took his knife and was about to kill his son.

But the angel of the Lord called to him from heaven. The angel said, "Abraham! Abraham!"

Abraham answered, "Yes."

The angel said, "Don't kill your son or hurt him in any way. Now I can see that you respect God. I see that you have not kept your son, your only son, from me."

Then Abraham looked up and saw a male sheep. Its horns were caught in a bush. So Abraham went and took the sheep and killed it. He offered it as a whole burnt offering to God. So Abraham named that place The Lord Gives. Even today people say, "On the mountain of the Lord it will be given."

The angel of the Lord called to Abraham from heaven a second time. The angel said, "The Lord says, 'You did not keep back your son, your only son, from me. Because you did this, I make you this promise by my own name: I will surely bless you and give you many descendants. They will be as many as the stars in the sky and the sand on the seashore. And they will capture the cities of their enemies. Through your descendants all the nations on the earth will be blessed. This is because you obeyed me.'"

Then Abraham returned to his servants. They all traveled back to Beersheba, and Abraham stayed there.

from Genesis 22:1–19

The Birth
of Moses

Most of the people of Israel lived in Egypt, and there were a lot of them. A new king came to power, and he didn't like the Israelites. He said: "Look! The people of Israel are too many! And they are too strong for us to handle!"

The Israelites were forced to work harder in order to wear

them down. But this made the Israelites grow in number and spread more. So the Egyptians became more afraid of them. They forced the Israelites to work even harder. The Egyptians made life hard for the Israelites.

There were two Hebrew nurses named Shiphrah and Puah. These nurses helped the Israelite women give birth to their babies. The king of Egypt said to the nurses, "When you are helping the Hebrew women give birth to their babies, watch! If the baby is a girl, let the baby live. But if it is a boy, kill it!" But the nurses

31

feared God. So they did not do as the king told them. They let all the boy babies live. Then the king of Egypt sent for the nurses. He said, "Why did you do this? Why did you let the boys live?"

The nurses said to him, "The Hebrew women are much stronger than the Egyptian women. They give birth to their babies before we can get there." God was good to the nurses. And the Hebrew people continued to grow in number. So they became even stronger. Because the nurses feared God, he gave them families of their own.

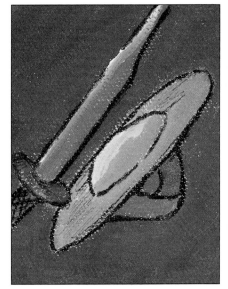

So the king commanded all his people: "Every time a boy is born to the Hebrews, you must throw him into the Nile River. But let all the girl babies live."

A married Israelite man and woman had a beautiful baby boy. Unable to keep him hidden after three months, the mother, Jochebed, made a basket, put the baby inside the basket, and put the basket among the tall grass at the edge of the Nile River. The baby's sister stood a short distance away. She wanted to see what would happen to him.

At about this time one of the king's daughters came down with her women to bathe at the river. She saw the basket in the tall grass. So she sent her slave girl to get it. The king's daughter opened the basket and saw the baby boy. He was crying, and she felt sorry for him. She said, "This is one of the Hebrew babies."

Then the baby's sister asked the king's daughter, "Would you like me to find a Hebrew woman to nurse the baby for you?"

The king's daughter said, "Yes, please."

So Miriam brought the baby's mother, Jochebed, to the king's daughter.

So the woman took her baby and nursed him. After the child had grown older, the woman took him to the king's daughter. She adopted the baby as her own son. The king's daughter named him Moses,[n] because the name Moses means "pulled from the water."

from Exodus 1:6–10, 15–22; 2:1–10

[n]**Moses** The name Moses sounds like the Hebrew word for "to pull out."   *33*

Moses and Zipporah

Because the daughter of the Egyptian king had saved him, Moses lived with the Egyptians as he was growing up. He dressed and acted like an Egyptian, but he was still a Hebrew.

Moses grew and became a man. One day he visited his peo-

ple, the Hebrews. He saw that they were forced to work very hard. He saw an Egyptian beating a Hebrew man, one of Moses' own people. Moses looked all around and saw that no one was watching. So he killed the Egyptian and hid his body in the sand.

The next day Moses returned and saw two Hebrew men fighting each other. He saw that one man was in the wrong. Moses said to that man, "Why are you hitting one of your own people?"

The man answered, "Who made you our ruler and judge? Are you going to kill me as you killed the Egyptian?"

Then Moses was afraid. He thought, "Now everyone knows what I did."

When the king heard about what Moses had done, he tried to kill Moses. But Moses ran away from the king and went to live in the land of Midian. Many of the people of Midian, who were descendants of Noah's son Ham, were shepherds. There Moses sat down near a well.

There was a priest in Midian who had seven daughters. His daughters went to that well to get water for their father's sheep. They were trying to fill the water troughs for their father's sheep. But some shepherds came and chased the girls away. Then Moses defended the girls and watered their sheep.

Then they went back to their father, Reuel, also called Jethro. He asked them, "Why have you come home so early today?"

The girls answered, "The shepherds chased us away. But an Egyptian defended us. He got water for us and watered our sheep."

He asked his daughters, "Where is this man? Why did you leave him? Invite him to eat with us."

Moses agreed to stay with Jethro. And he gave his daughter Zipporah to Moses to be his wife. Zipporah gave birth to a son, and Moses named him Gershom.[n] Moses named him this because Moses was a stranger in a land that was not his own. The name Gershom means "foreigner."

Now in those times, it was the law of God that all boys must be circumcised before they were eight days old. This meant cutting a small flap of their skin, which meant that they worshiped the Lord God. To not circumcise your baby boy meant you were denying that you belonged to God.

Because Moses was unable to circumcise their son, Zipporah worried that the Lord would kill Moses. **But Zipporah took a flint knife and circumcised her son. She took the skin and touched Moses' feet with it. Then she said to him, "You are a bridegroom of blood to me."** What she meant was that because she had circumcised the boy, she had done what God had ordered Moses to do. Now both her son and her husband would no longer be out of God's favor.

from Exodus 2:11–23; 4:24–26

"Gershom This name sounds like the Hebrew name meaning "a stranger there."

The Exodus

The Israelites complained because they were forced to be slaves. They cried out to the Lord for help, and God heard their loud cries. He did not forget the promise he had made to Abraham, Isaac and Jacob about the Israelite people.

The Lord decided to send Moses to free his people from Egypt. The Lord appeared to Moses in a burning bush. God said to

Moses: "I have seen the troubles my people have suffered in Egypt. And I have heard their cries when the Egyptian slave masters hurt them. I am concerned about their pain. I have come down to save them from the Egyptians. I will bring them out of that land. I will lead them to a good land with lots of room. This is a land where much food grows. So now I am sending you to the king of Egypt. Go! Bring my people, the Israelites, out of Egypt!"

But Moses said to God, "I am not a great man! Why should I be the one to go to the king and lead the Israelites out of Egypt?"

God said, "I will be with you."

Moses, along with his brother Aaron, did as the Lord commanded and went to Egypt. Unfortunately, the king refused to let the Israelite slaves go. He was a very stubborn king. Only after God sent ten different types of troubles for him and his people did the king finally decide to let the Israelites go.

"Get up and leave my people. You and your people may do as you have asked. Go and worship the Lord. Take all of your sheep and cattle as you have asked. Go."

The Israelites, led by Moses, walked out of Egypt and began their journey through the desert to the land the Lord had promised.

The king of Egypt was told that the people of Israel had already left. Then he and his officers changed their minds about them. They realized they no longer had their obedient slaves to work for them.

So the king prepared his war chariot and took his army with him. They were going after Moses and the Israelite caravan to return them to Egypt.

The Israelites were camping by the Red Sea. When they saw the king coming with his army of at least six hundred chariots, they were very frightened and cried to the Lord for help. They said to Moses, "What have you done to us? Why did you bring us out of Egypt to die in the desert? There were plenty of graves for us in Egypt. We told you in Egypt, 'Let us alone! Let us stay and serve the Egyptians.' Now we will die in the desert."

But Moses answered, "Don't be afraid! Stand still and see the Lord save you today. You will never see these Egyptians again after today. You will only need to remain calm. The Lord will fight for you."

Then the Lord said to Moses, "Why are you crying out to me? Command the people of Israel to start moving. Raise your walking stick and hold it over the sea. The sea will split. Then the people can cross the sea on dry land. I have made the Egyptians stubborn so they will chase the Israelites. But I will be honored when I defeat the king and all of his chariot drivers and chariots."

A large cloud moved between the Egyptians and the Israelites. The cloud gave light for the Israelites and darkness for the Egyptians.

Moses held his hand over the sea. All that night the Lord drove back the sea with a strong east wind. And so he made the sea become dry ground. The water was split. And the Israelites went through the sea on dry land. A wall of water was on both sides.

Then all the king's horses, chariots and chariot drivers followed them into the sea. When all the Israelites made it to the other side, the Lord instructed Moses to again stretch his arms across the sea. The walls of water came down and covered the Egyptians. Not one soldier remained alive.

On that day the Israelites knew that the Lord had saved them, and they worshiped the Lord and trusted his servant Moses.

from **Exodus 3—14**

Jethro

Jethro was a descendant of Ham, and he was a kind, just and wise Midianite priest. He was the father of Moses' wife, Zipporah. Moses and Zipporah had met while she was watching her father's sheep; so Jethro was a shepherd as well as a good priest for God.

Jethro understood how important it is to do the things that

God asks us to do. When he saw that his son-in-law, Moses, had been called to greatness on behalf of the Lord, Jethro did everything he could to help Moses fulfill his purpose. He had heard about everything that God had done for Moses and his people, the Israelites. Jethro heard how the Lord had led the Israelites out of Egypt.

Moses had sent his wife Zipporah to Jethro, his father-in-law. Moses had also sent his two sons. Jethro watched over them during the time when Moses was leading the Israelites out of **43**

Egypt. While Moses and the people of Israel were camped near Mount Sinai, Jethro had sent a message ahead to Moses. He said, "I am Jethro, your father-in-law. I am coming to you with your wife and her two sons."

So Moses went out to meet his father-in-law. Moses bowed down and then kissed him. The two men asked about each other's health. Then they went into Moses' tent. Moses told his father-in-law everything the Lord had done to the king and the Egyptians. The Lord had done these things to help Israel. Moses told about all the problems they had  faced along the way. And Moses told him how the Lord had saved them.

Jethro was very happy when he heard all the good things the Lord had done for Israel. He was happy because the Lord had saved them from the Egyptians. Jethro said, "Praise the Lord. He has saved all of you from the Egyptians and their king. He has saved the people from the power of the Egyptians. Now I know the Lord is greater than all gods. He did this to those who looked down on Israel."

The next day Moses solved disagreements among the people. So the people stood around Moses from morning until night. Moses' father-in-law saw all that Moses was doing for the people. He asked, "What is all this you are doing for the people? Why are you the only one to solve disagreements? All the people are standing around you from morning until night!"

Then Moses said to his father-in-law, "It is because the people come to me for God's help in solving their disagreements. When people have a disagreement, they come to me. I decide who is right. And I tell them God's laws and teachings."

Moses' father-in-law said to him, "You are not doing this right. You and the people who come to you will get too tired. This is too much work for you. You can't do it by yourself. Now listen to me. I will give you some advice. I want God to be with you. You must talk to God for the people. You must tell him about their disagreements. You should tell them the laws and teachings. Tell them the right way to live and what they should do.

You will need to choose some leaders who love God and are honest. They can bring the hard cases to you. But they can decide the simple cases themselves.

Moses followed Jethro's advice and appointed other leaders to help him. Then Jethro, the wise advisor and priest, returned home.

from **Exodus 18:1–22, 24, 25, 27**

The Ten Commandments

Moses led the Israelites out of Egypt. After traveling for two months, they set up camp in the desert at the foot of Mount Sinai.

Then Moses went up on the mountain to God. The Lord called to him from the mountain. The Lord said, "Say this to the family of Jacob. And tell this to the people of Israel: 'Every one of

you has seen what I did to the people of Egypt. You saw how I carried you out of Egypt. I did it as an eagle carries her young on her wings. And I brought you here to me. So now obey me and keep my agreement. Do this, and you will be my own possession, chosen from all nations. Even though the whole earth is mine, you will be my kingdom of priests. You will be a nation that belongs to me alone.'"

Moses went back down the mountain and told the people what God had said and they promised to do everything the Lord

47

commanded. The people gathered at the foot of the mountain to hear God's words.

There was thunder and lightning with a thick cloud on the mountain. And there was a very loud blast from a trumpet. Smoke

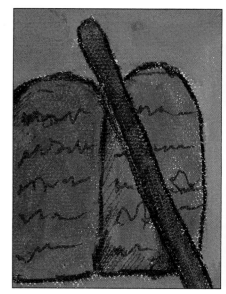

rose from the mountain like smoke from a furnace. And the whole mountain shook wildly. The sound of the trumpet became louder. Then Moses spoke, and the voice of God answered him.

Then God spoke all these words:

"I am the Lord your God. I brought you out of the land of Egypt where you were slaves.

1. "You must not have any other gods except me.

2. "Don't make something that looks like anything in the sky above or on the earth below or in the water below the land. You must not worship or serve any idol.

3. "You must not use the name of the Lord your God thoughtlessly.

4. "Remember to keep the Sabbath as a holy day. You may work and get everything done during six days each week. But the seventh day is a day of rest to honor the Lord your God. On that day no one may do any work.

5. "Honor your father and your mother.

6. "You must not murder anyone.

7. "You must not be guilty of adultery.

8. "You must not steal.

9. "You must not tell lies about your neighbor in court.

10. "You must not want to take anything that belongs to your neighbor."

The people heard the thunder and the trumpet. They saw the lightning on the mountain and smoke rising from the mountain. They shook with fear and stood far away from the mountain. Then they said to Moses, "Speak to us yourself. Then we will listen. But don't let God speak to us or we will die."

Then Moses said to the people, "Don't be afraid. God has come to test you. He wants you to respect him so you will not sin." He explained how important it was that the people obey God.

The people stood far away from the mountain while Moses went near the dark cloud where God was. Then the Lord told Moses to say these things to the Israelites: "You yourselves have seen that I talked with you from heaven. You must not use gold or silver to make idols for yourselves. You must not worship these false gods in addition to me."

from **Exodus 19:1–6, 14–19; 20:1–23**

Joshua and the Walls of Jericho

Joshua was chosen by God to lead Israel across the Jordan River and into the land that God had promised them. God told Joshua, "Be strong and brave! Be sure to obey all the teachings my servant Moses gave you. So don't be afraid. The Lord your God will be with you everywhere you go."

Joshua was near Jericho. He looked up and saw a man standing in front of him. The man had a sword in his hand. Joshua went to him and asked, "Are you a friend or an enemy?"

The man answered, "I am neither one. I have come as the commander of the Lord's army."

Then Joshua bowed facedown on the ground. He asked, "Does my master have a command for me, his servant?"

The commander of the Lord's army answered, "Take off **51**

your sandals. The place where you are standing is holy." So Joshua did.

Now the people of Jericho were afraid because the Israelites were near. So they closed the city gates and guarded them. No one went into the city. And no one came out.

Then the Lord spoke to Joshua. He said, "Look, I have given you Jericho, its king and all its fighting men. March around the city with your army one time every day. Do this for six days. Have seven priests carry trumpets made from horns of male sheep. Tell them to march

in front of the Holy Box. On the seventh day march around the city seven times. On that day tell the priests to blow the trumpets as they march. They will make one long blast on the trumpets. When you hear that sound, have all the people give a loud shout. Then the walls of the city will fall. And the people will go straight into the city."

Joshua and the Israelites did as the Lord commanded. And, on the seventh day when the priests blew the trumpets, the people shouted. At the sound of the trumpets and the people's shout, the walls fell. And everyone ran straight into the city. So the Israelites defeated that city. They killed everyone in Jericho, even the animals.

Then Israel burned the whole city and everything in it. But they did not burn the things made from silver, gold, bronze and iron. These were saved for the Lord.

So the Lord was with Joshua because Joshua was loyal and faithful.

from **Joshua 1:6–9; 5:13–15; 6:1–27**

Gideon

There was peace in the land for 40 years. Then again the people of Israel did what the Lord said was wrong. So for seven years the Lord let the people of Midian rule Israel. The Midianites were very powerful and were cruel to the Israelites. So the Israelites made hiding places in the mountains. They also hid in caves and safe places. Whenever the Israelites planted crops, the

Midianites, Amalekites and other peoples from the east would come and attack them. The Midianites came up and camped in the land. They brought their tents and their animals with them. They were like swarms of locusts! There were so many people and camels they could not be counted. These people came into the land to ruin it.

One day an angel of the Lord appeared to Gideon, an Israelite, and said, "The Lord is with you, mighty warrior!"

Then Gideon said, "Pardon me, sir. If the Lord is with us,

why are we having so many troubles? He has allowed the Midianites to defeat us."

The Lord turned to Gideon and said, "You have the strength to save the people of Israel. Go and save them from the Midianites. I am the one who is sending you."

But Gideon answered, "Pardon me, Lord. How can I save Israel? My family group is the weakest in Manasseh. And I am the least important member of my family."

The Lord answered him, "I will be with you. It will seem as if you are fighting only one man."

Gideon was finally ready for battle. The spirit of the Lord entered Gideon! Gideon blew a trumpet to call the Abiezrites to follow him.

Then Gideon said to God, "You said you would help me save Israel. I will put some wool on the threshing floor. Let there be dew only on the wool. But let all of the ground be dry. Then I will know what you said is true." And that is just what happened.

Then the Lord said to Gideon, "You have too many men to defeat the Midianites. I don't want the Israelites to brag that they saved themselves." So Gideon's troops were cut from 35,000 men to only 10,000 men.

Then the Lord said to Gideon, "There are still too many men." So Gideon's troops were cut to just 300 men.

Gideon and his soldiers blew their trumpets, shouting "Fight for the Lord," and the Lord caused all the men of Midian to fight each other with their swords! The enemy army ran away but the Israelites chased them, and eventually the army was destroyed.

The Lord created a plan for Gideon that would let him successfully conquer the Midianites. Gideon did just as the Lord told him, and the Midianites were defeated.

from **Judges 5:31—7:22**

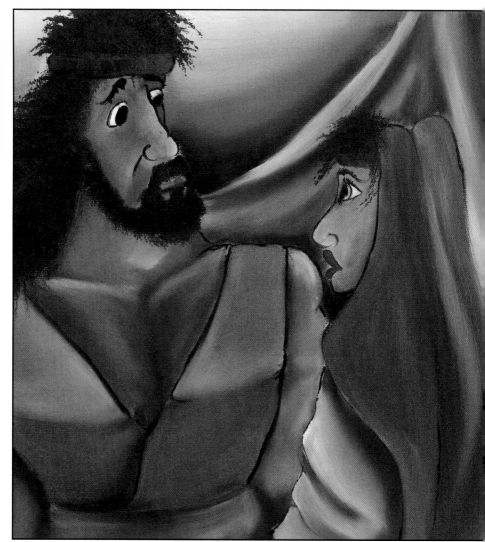

Samson
and Delilah

Samson was a strong and powerful man. As a young boy he had been blessed by the Lord with extraordinary strength. Once he tore a lion apart with his bare hands!

The Philistines hated Samson because he had used his strength to kill many of them. They wanted to take their revenge,

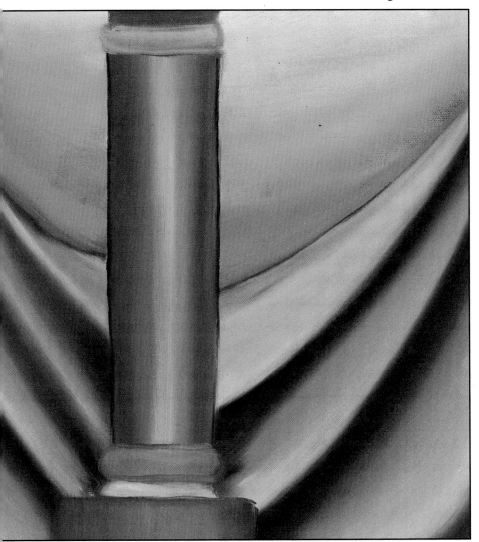

but first they needed to find the secret to his enormous strength. What made Samson so powerful?

After this, Samson fell in love with a woman named Delilah. She lived in the Valley of Sorek. The kings of the Philistines went to Delilah and offered her money to find out the secret to Samson's strength.

So Delilah said to Samson, "Tell me why you are so strong. How could someone tie you up and take control of you?"

Samson answered, "Someone would have to tie me up. He   *59* would have to use seven new bowstrings that have not been dried. If he did that, I would be as weak as any other man."

This was not true, and when Delilah tied him up, Samson easily broke the bowstrings. They broke like pieces of string burned in a fire. Delilah was angry, and begged Samson to tell her his secret. Because he didn't want to tell his secret, Samson fooled Delilah again and again, never revealing the secret of his strength. But Delilah nagged and pestered until Samson could stand it no longer.

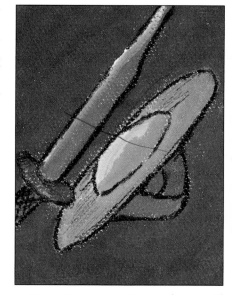

So he told her everything. He said, "I have never had my hair cut. I have been set apart to God as a Nazirite since I was born. If someone shaved my head, then I would lose my strength. I would become as weak as any other man."

Delilah saw that he had told her everything sincerely. So she sent a message to the kings of the Philistines. Then she invited Samson back to her house.

With Samson asleep on her lap, she began cutting his hair. When she finished, she tied him up and shouted, "Samson, the Philistines are about to capture you!"

He woke up and thought, "I'll get loose as I did before and shake myself free." But he did not know that the Lord had left him.

Then the Philistines captured Samson. They tore out his eyes. And they took him down to Gaza. They put bronze chains on him. They put him in prison and made him grind grain. But his hair began to grow again.

One night the Philistine rulers threw a big party. They were celebrating in a temple packed with three thousand or more people. The rulers brought Samson out of prison, and everyone began making fun of him.

Then Samson prayed to the Lord. He said, "Lord God, remember me. God, please give me strength one more time." Then Samson held the two center pillars of the temple. These two pillars supported the whole temple. Samson said, "Let me die with these Philistines!" Then he pushed as hard as he could. And the temple fell on the kings and all the people in it. So Samson killed more of the Philistines when he died than when he was alive.

from **Judges 16:4–25, 27–30**

Ruth and Naomi

L ong ago the judges[n] ruled Israel. During their rule, there was a
time in the land when there was not enough food to eat. A man
named Elimelech left Bethlehem in Judah and moved to the country
of Moab. He took his wife and his two sons with him. His wife was
named Naomi, and his two sons were named Mahlon and Kilion.

Later, Naomi's husband, Elimelech, died. So only Naomi and

her two sons were left. These sons married women from Moab. The name of one wife was Orpah. The name of the other wife was Ruth. Naomi and her sons lived in Moab about ten years. Then Mahlon and Kilion also died. So Naomi was left alone without her husband or her two sons.

While Naomi was in Moab, she heard that the Lord had taken care of his people. He had given food to them in Judah. So Naomi got ready to leave Moab and go back home. The wives of Naomi's sons also got ready to go with her. So they left the place where they had lived. And they started back on the way to the land of Judah. But Naomi said to her two daughters-in-law, "Go back home. Each of you go to your own mother's house. You have been very kind to me and to my sons who are now dead. I hope the Lord will also be kind to you in the same way. I hope the Lord will give you another home and a new husband."

Then Naomi kissed the women. The daughters-in-law still wanted to go with Naomi. They loved her very much. Naomi tried to explain that it was best that they return to their own families.

"My life is much too hard for you to share. This is because the Lord is against me!" Naomi told them. She believed the women had a better chance at a new life without her.

The women cried, but finally Orpah kissed her mother-in-law goodbye. Ruth did not. She again pleaded with Naomi. Ruth told Naomi that she'd follow Naomi wherever she would go. She vowed to be by Naomi's side forever.

Naomi saw that Ruth had made up her mind to go with her. So Naomi stopped arguing with her. Naomi and Ruth went on until they came to the town of Bethlehem. When the two women entered Bethlehem, all the people became very excited.

Ruth went out to find work, and she found a job picking up grain in a field owned by a man named Boaz, who was a rich man living in Bethlehem. **Boaz was one of Naomi's close relatives from** Elimelech's family. Boaz had heard how Ruth helped her mother-in-law, so he made Ruth's work easier. He also made sure that no one would treat or speak harshly to Ruth.

So Ruth continued working closely with the women servants of Boaz. She gathered grain until the barley harvest was finished. She also worked there through the end of the wheat harvest. And Ruth continued to live with Naomi, her mother-in-law.

Then Naomi, Ruth's mother-in-law, said to her, "My daughter, I must find a suitable home for you. That would be good for you. Now Boaz is our close relative.[n] You worked with his women servants." She told Ruth to go to Boaz and remind him that it was his duty to take care of his kinfolk.

Then Boaz said, "The Lord bless you, my daughter. Your kindness to me is greater than the kindness you showed to Naomi in the beginning. You didn't look for a young man to marry, either rich or poor. Now, my daughter, don't be afraid. I will do everything you ask. All the people in our town know you are a very good woman.

Boaz went and bought Naomi's property, and he married Ruth so that he could take care of both of them. The Lord blessed Ruth with a son. After his birth, the women told Naomi, "Praise the Lord who gave you this grandson. And may he become famous in Israel. He will give you new life. And he will take care of you in your old age."

And he did. The baby boy was named Obed, and he was the grandfather of the greatest king of all Israel, King David.

from **Ruth 1—4**

---

[n]**judges** They were not judges in courts of law, but leaders of the people in times of emergency.

[n]**close relative** In Bible times the closest relative could marry a widow without children so she could have children. He would care for this family, but they and their property would not belong to him. They would belong to the dead husband.

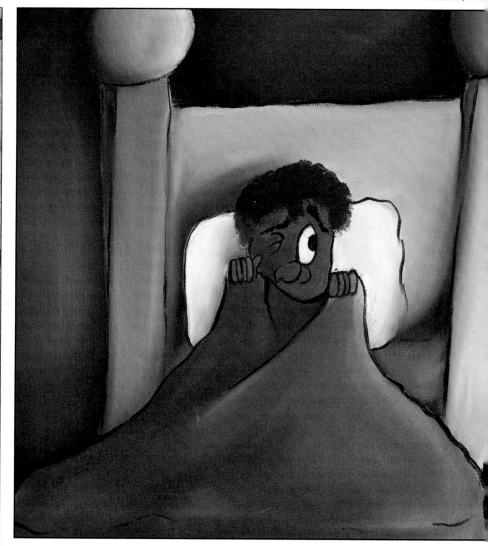

Samuel in the Temple

Elkanah and Hannah desperately wanted a child. Every year Elkanah left his town Ramah and went up to Shiloh. There he worshiped the Lord of heaven's armies and offered sacrifices to him. There Hannah prayed that the Lord would bless her with a son.

One time when Elkanah and Hannah went to Shiloh, Han-

nah was crying as she prayed because she was so brokenhearted. She said, "Lord of heaven's armies, see how bad I feel. Remember me! Don't forget me. If you will give me a son, I will give him back to you all his life."

Eli was one of the Lord's priests there, and he heard Hannah praying. Eli said to her, "Go in peace. May the God of Israel give you what you asked of him."

So Hannah became pregnant, and in time she gave birth to a son. His name was Samuel. Just as Hannah had promised, when

67

Samuel was a little older she gave her son back to the Lord. Samuel stayed in the temple in Shiloh with Eli and served the Lord.

The boy Samuel served the Lord under Eli. In those days the Lord did not speak directly to people very often. There were very few visions.

Eli's eyes were so weak he was almost blind. One night he was lying in bed. Samuel was also in bed in the Lord's Holy Tent.

Then the Lord called Samuel. Samuel answered, "I am here!" He ran to Eli and said, "I am here. You called me."

But Eli said, "I didn't call you. Go back to bed." So Samuel went back to bed.

The Lord called again, "Samuel!" Samuel again went to Eli and said, "I am here. You called me."

Again Eli said, "I didn't call you. Go back to bed."

Samuel did not yet know the Lord. The Lord had not spoken directly to him yet.

The Lord called Samuel for the third time. Samuel got up and went to Eli. He said, "I am here. You called me."

Then Eli realized the Lord was calling the boy. So he told Samuel, "Go to bed. If he calls you again, say, 'Speak, Lord. I am your servant, and I am listening.'" So Samuel went and lay down in bed.

Then the Lord came and stood there. He called as he had before. He said, "Samuel, Samuel!"

Samuel said, "Speak, Lord. I am your servant, and I am listening."

The Lord said to Samuel, "See, I am going to do something in Israel. It will shock those who hear about it. At that time I will do to Eli and his family everything I promised. I will not stop until

I have finished. I told Eli I would punish his family forever. I will do it because Eli knew his sons were evil. They spoke against me, but he did not control them. So here is what I promised Eli's family: 'Your guilt will never be removed by sacrifice or offering.'"

Samuel lay down until morning. Then he opened the doors of the Tent of the Lord. He was afraid to tell Eli about the vision. But Eli said to him, "Samuel, my son!"

Samuel answered, "I am here."

Eli asked, "What did the Lord say to you? Don't hide it from me. May God punish you terribly if you hide from me anything he said to you." So Samuel told Eli everything. He did not hide anything from him. Then Eli said, "He is the Lord. Let him do what he thinks is best."

The Lord was with Samuel as he grew up. He did not let any of Samuel's messages fail to come true.

from **1 Samuel 1; 3**

David and Goliath

David lived near Bethlehem with his father, Jesse, and his seven brothers. The Lord had chosen him to be special, and the Spirit of the Lord took control of him.

The enemies of Israel at that time were the Philistines. The Philistines gathered their armies for war. The Israelites, under the

command of King Saul, set up camp on a hill near the Philistine camp.

The Philistines had a champion fighter named Goliath. He was from Gath. He was about nine feet four inches tall. He came out of the Philistine camp. He had a bronze helmet on his head. And he wore a coat of scale armor. It was made of bronze and weighed about 125 pounds. He wore bronze protectors on his legs. And he had a small spear of bronze tied on his back. The wooden part of his larger spear was like a weaver's rod. And its blade weighed about 15 pounds.

Goliath stood and shouted to the Israelite soldiers, "Why have you taken positions for battle? I am a Philistine, and you are Saul's servants! Choose a man and send him to fight me. If he can fight and kill me, we will become your servants. But if I defeat and kill him, you will become our servants." Then he said, "Today I stand and dare the army of Israel! Send one of your men to fight me!" When Saul and the Israelites heard the Philistine's words, they were very afraid.

Now David was the son of Jesse, an Ephrathite. David was the youngest son. Jesse's three oldest sons followed Saul. But David went back and forth from Saul to Bethlehem. There he took care of his father's sheep.

Now Jesse said to his son David, "Take this half bushel of cooked grain. And take ten loaves of bread. Take them to your brothers in the camp."

Early in the morning David left the sheep with another shepherd. He took the food and left as Jesse had told him. While he was in the army camp, Goliath came out. He was the Philistine champion from Gath. He shouted things against Israel as usual, and David heard it and asked why no one had gone to fight Goliath.

Some men heard what David said and told Saul. Then Saul ordered David to be sent to him and David offered to fight the giant.

Saul answered, "You can't go out against this Philistine and fight him. You're only a boy. Goliath has been a warrior since he was a young man."

But David said to Saul, "The Lord saved me from a lion and a bear. He will also save me from this Philistine."

Saul agreed to let David fight the giant. He even offered David his armor. But David refused it, taking only his sling and five smooth rocks.

Goliath looked at David. He saw that David was only a boy, tanned and handsome. He looked down at David with disgust. He said to David, "Come here. I'll feed your body to the birds of the air and the wild animals!"

But David said to him, "You come to me using a sword, a large spear and a small spear. But I come to you in the name of the Lord of heaven's armies."

As Goliath came near to attack him, David ran quickly to meet him. He took a stone from his pouch. He put it into his sling and slung it. The stone hit the Philistine on his forehead and sank into it. Goliath fell facedown on the ground.

So David defeated the Philistine with only a sling and a stone!

As David said, those who love God must never forget that the Lord does not need swords or spears to save people. The battle belongs to him!

from **1 Samuel 16; 17**

The Ethiopian Messenger

King David's son, Absalom, rebelled against his father and caused the Israelites to turn against the king's men in battle. David loved his son Absalom even though he had disobeyed and done wrong. Despite their differences, David made it clear that no one was to harm Absalom.

When Absalom saw that he would be defeated, he ran. As Absalom was riding his mule, it went under a large oak tree. The branches were thick, and Absalom's head got caught in the tree. His mule ran out from under him. So Absalom was left hanging above the ground. Some of David's soldiers saw him and told Joab, who was in charge of David's army.

Joab said to him, "You saw him? Why didn't you kill him and let him fall to the ground?"

The man answered, "I wouldn't try to hurt the king's son. We heard the king's command to you, Abishai and Ittai. The king said, 'Be careful not to hurt young Absalom.'"

Joab was angry, and despite the king's orders, Joab killed Absalom for his rebellion against David.

Ahimaaz son of Zadok spoke to Joab. He said, "Let me run and take the news to King David. I'll tell him the Lord has destroyed the enemy for him."

But Joab knew that Ahimaaz only wanted to tell David in order to get attention. Joab answered Ahimaaz, "No, you are not the one to take the news today. You may do it another time. But do not take it today."

An Ethiopian messenger was standing nearby. His tall, black, shiny body looked as if it were made for running. Everyone knew of his great running abilities. Joab told him, "Go. Tell the king what you have seen." The Cushite bowed to Joab and ran to tell David.

But Ahimaaz son of Zadok begged Joab again. He said, "No matter what happens, please let me go, along with the Cushite!"

Joab explained to Ahimaaz that he'd receive no reward for telling the king the news.

Ahimaaz answered, "No matter what happens, I will run."

Joab finally agreed and let Ahimaaz run, too. Then Ahimaaz ran by way of the Jordan Valley and passed the Cushite.

Now David was sitting between the inner and outer gates of the city. The watchman went up to the roof by the gate walls. As he looked up, he saw a man running alone. He shouted to tell King David.

The king said, "If he is alone, he is bringing good news!"

The man came nearer and nearer to the city. Then the

watchman saw another man running. The watchman called to the gatekeeper, "Look! Another man is running alone!"

The king said, "He is also bringing good news!"

The watchman said, "I think the first man runs like Ahimaaz son of Zadok."

The king said, "Ahimaaz is a good man. He must be bringing good news!"

Then Ahimaaz called a greeting to the king. He bowed face-down on the ground to the king. He said, "Praise the Lord your God! The Lord has defeated the men who were against you, my king."

The king asked, "Is young Absalom all right?"

Ahimaaz answered, "When Joab sent me, I saw some great excitement. But I don't know what it was."

Then the king said, "Step over here and wait." So Ahimaaz stepped aside and stood there.

Then the Cushite arrived. He said, "Master and king, hear the good news! Today the Lord has punished the people who were against you!"

The king asked the Cushite, "Is young Absalom all right?"

The Cushite answered, "May your enemies be like that young man. May all who come to hurt you be like that young man!"

Then the king knew Absalom was dead. He was very upset. He went to the room over the city gate and cried.

Ahimaaz had wanted the king's attention, but he refused to tell David the whole truth. Only the Ethiopian messenger had the courage to carry the bad news to the king.

***from* 2 Samuel 18:9–33a**

The Queen of Sheba

King Solomon was a very rich king, and he was considered the wisest man in the world. The country of Israel was more important than ever before because of King Solomon.

The Queen of Sheba was a very beautiful and rich queen,

who ruled a country to the south of Israel. The land of Sheba was known for the wonderful things, such as perfumes and incense, that it sold to the royal courts of other countries.

The Queen of Sheba had heard about Solomon's fame. So she came to test him with hard questions. She traveled to Jerusalem with a very large group of servants. There were many camels carrying spices, jewels and much gold. She came to Solomon and talked with him about all that she had in mind. Solomon answered all her questions. Nothing was too hard for him to explain to her. The queen of Sheba learned that Solomon was very wise. She saw the palace he had built. She saw his many officers and the food on his table. She saw the palace servants and their good clothes. She was shown the servants who served him at

feasts. And she was shown the whole burnt offerings he made in the Temple of the Lord. All these things amazed her.

So she said to King Solomon, "I heard in my own country about your achievements and wisdom. And all of it is true. I could not believe it then. But now I have come and seen it with my own eyes. I was not told even the half of it! Your wisdom and wealth are much greater than I had heard. Your men and officers are very lucky! In always serving you, they are able to hear your wisdom! Praise the Lord your God! He was pleased to make you king of Israel. The Lord has constant love for Israel. So he made you king to keep justice and to rule fairly."

What a lesson this woman brings to us! Instead of being jealous and wanting what Solomon had, she praised God for all he had done for this wise king. She came from a country that was well-known for its treasures and spices, but she was pleased to see how God had blessed Solomon.

Then the queen of Sheba gave the king about 9,000 pounds of gold. She also gave him many spices and jewels. No one since that time has brought more spices into Israel than the queen of Sheba gave King Solomon.

King Solomon gave the queen of Sheba many gifts. He gave her gifts that a king would give to another ruler. Then he gave her whatever else she wanted and asked for.

from **1 Kings 10:1–13**

Elijah
and Elisha

Elijah was a great prophet of the Lord. He was obedient and did whatever the Lord asked him to do. He and Elisha traveled all over spreading the Lord's word.

One day Elijah said to Elisha, "Please stay here. The Lord has told me to go to Bethel." Elisha promised that he would stay with Elijah no matter what. So they went down to Bethel.

Elisha met a group of prophets in Bethel, and they asked him, "Do you know the Lord will take your master away from you today?"

Elisha said, "Yes, I know. But don't talk about it."

Elijah then told Elisha that the Lord wanted him to travel to Jericho. Again he told Elisha to stay behind. Elisha again

83

promised never to leave his teacher's side. He traveled to Jericho with Elijah.

A group of the prophets at Jericho came to Elisha. They said, "Do you know that the Lord will take your master away from you today?"

Elisha answered, "Yes, I know. But don't talk about it."

Elijah said to Elisha, "Stay here. The Lord has sent me to the Jordan River." Still again, Elisha promised never to leave Elijah. So the two of them walked on together.

Fifty men from a group of the prophets came. They stood far from where Elijah and Elisha were by the Jordan. Elijah took off his coat. Then he rolled it up and hit the water. The water divided to the right and to the left. Then Elijah and Elisha crossed over on dry ground.

After they had crossed over, Elijah said to Elisha, "What can I do for you before I am taken from you?"

Elisha said, "Leave me a double share of your spirit."[n]

Elijah said, "You have asked a hard thing. But if you see me when I am taken from you, it will be yours. If you don't, it won't happen."

Elijah and Elisha were still walking and talking. Then a chariot and horses of fire appeared. The chariot and horses of fire separated Elijah from Elisha. Then Elijah went up to heaven in a whirlwind. Elisha did not see him anymore. Elisha grabbed his own clothes and tore them to show how sad he was.

He picked up Elijah's coat that had fallen from him. Then Elisha returned and stood on the bank of the Jordan. Elisha hit the water with Elijah's coat. He said, "Where is the Lord, the God of Elijah?" When he hit the water, it divided to the right and to the left. Then Elisha crossed over.

A group of prophets at Jericho were watching. They said, "Elisha now has the spirit Elijah had." They came to meet him. And they bowed down to the ground before him.

from 2 Kings 2:1–11, 12b–15

[n]"Leave . . . spirit." By law, the first son in a family would inherit a double share of his father's possessions. Elisha is asking to inherit a share of his master's power. He is not asking for twice as much power as Elijah had.

The Healing of Naaman

Naaman was commander of the army of the king of Aram. He was a great man to his master. He had much honor because the Lord had used him to give victory to Aram. He was a mighty and brave man. But he had a harmful skin disease.

The Arameans had gone out to steal from the Israelites. And they had taken a little girl as a captive from Israel. This little girl served Naaman's wife. She said to her mistress, "I wish that my master would meet the prophet who lives in Samaria. He would heal Naaman of his disease." Clearly, God can use anyone, even a small girl, to give good news to those who need it.

So Naaman went with his horses and chariots to Elisha's house. And he stood outside the door.

Elisha sent a messenger to Naaman. The messenger said, "Go and wash in the Jordan River seven times. Then your skin will be healed, and you will be clean."

Naaman became angry and left. He said, "I thought Elisha would surely come out and stand before me. I thought he would call on the name of the Lord his God. I thought he would wave his hand over the place and heal the disease! Abana and Pharpar, the rivers of Damascus, are better than all the waters of Israel! Why can't I wash in them and become clean?"

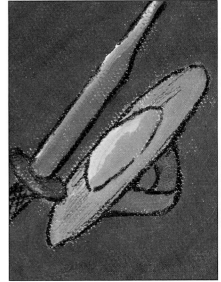

But Naaman's servants came near and talked to him. They said, "My father, if the prophet had told you to do some great thing, wouldn't you have done it? Doesn't it make more sense just to do it? After all, he only told you, 'Wash, and you will be clean.'"

Naaman recognized this wisdom. He had not been told to do something hard in order to be healed. He needed only to obey.

Like Naaman, many of us think that obeying God means doing something hard. But just as Naaman was told to do something simple—wash in the river—we can obey God by doing simple things like praying, reading our Bible, keeping our promises and believing that Jesus Christ is God's son. Obeying God is not hard. Naaman found this out, too.

So Naaman went down and dipped in the Jordan seven times. He did just as Elisha had said. Then Naaman's skin became new again. It was like the skin of a little boy. And Naaman was

clean!

Naaman and all his group came back to Elisha. He stood before Elisha and said, "Look. I now know there is no God in all the earth except in Israel!"

Naaman offered gifts to thank Elisha, but Elisha would not take them. He wanted Naaman to know that God had been the one who healed him, and he wanted Naaman to give gifts to the Lord. Naaman promised Elisha that he would give offerings only to the Lord from then on.

from **2 Kings 5:1–12a, 13–17**

Nehemiah

Nehemiah was a Jewish man who worked for the king. He was in charge of all the wine used at the king's table. The king trusted and depended upon Nehemiah to keep careful watch over all his meals. This job made it possible for Nehemiah to see the king every day.

One day Nehemiah's brother came for a visit. He asked his

brother how things were in Jerusalem. Nehemiah's brother sadly told him the poor conditions of Jerusalem. The walls were all broken down, and the gates had been burned.

When Nehemiah heard all this, he sat down and cried. For days he mourned. He went without eating to show his sorrow and prayed: "Lord, God of heaven, you are the great God who is to be respected. You keep your agreement of love with those who love you and obey your commands.

"Lord, listen carefully to my prayer. . . . Give me, your

servant, success today. Allow this king to show kindness to me."

Later, when Nehemiah served wine to the king, the king noticed how sad Nehemiah looked. So the king said, "Why does your face look sad? You are not sick. Your heart must be sad."

Nehemiah, frightened, answered, "May the king live forever! My face is sad because the city where my ancestors are buried lies in ruins. And its gates have been destroyed by fire."

Then the king said to him, "What do you want?"

First, Nehemiah prayed to God in heaven, then told the king, "Send me to the city in Judah where my ancestors are buried. I will rebuild it. Do this if you are willing and if I have pleased you." The king agreed and sent Nehemiah back to Judah. He even prepared letters to the governors of all the places Nehemiah would travel through. This was to make sure Nehemiah would have a safe trip to Judah and a safe return. The king also sent along army officers and cavalry troops.

Nehemiah and his group set off for Judah. Sanballat and Tobiah heard about what happened and were very angry. They were upset that someone had come to help the Israelites.

Nehemiah went to Jerusalem and stayed there three days. Then at night he started out with a few men.

Nehemiah was inspecting the walls of Jerusalem. They had been broken down. And the gates had been destroyed by fire. When he returned, he told the officials, "You can see the trouble we have here. Jerusalem is a pile of ruins. And its gates have been burned. Come, let's rebuild the wall of Jerusalem. Then we won't be full of shame any longer."

When Sanballat and Tobiah heard Nehemiah's plan to rebuild, they tore down his ideas with insults saying, "What are you doing? Are you turning against the king?"

Nehemiah answered, "The God of heaven will give us success. We are God's servants."

Everyone helped rebuild the wall. When it was complete, Sanballat and Tobiah sent a message to Nehemiah asking him to meet them. Nehemiah sent a message back, "I am doing a great work. I can't come down. I don't want the work to stop while I leave to meet you." Sanballat and Geshem sent the same message to Nehemiah four times. And he sent back the same answer each time.

The fifth time Sanballat sent his helper to Nehemiah with the message. And in his hand was an unsealed letter. This is what was written: "A report is going around to all the nations. . . . It says you and the Jews are planning to turn against the king. That's why you are rebuilding the wall. They say you are going to be their king."

Nehemiah sent him back this answer: "Nothing you are saying is really happening. You are just making it up in your own mind."

Sanballat was indeed only trying to frighten Nehemiah. None of his claims were true. Nehemiah prayed to the Lord, "Remember Tobiah and Sanballat. Remember what they have done."

The wall was completely rebuilt. When the enemies in the surrounding nations learned that the work was finished, they felt helpless, because they knew that God had helped rebuild the wall.

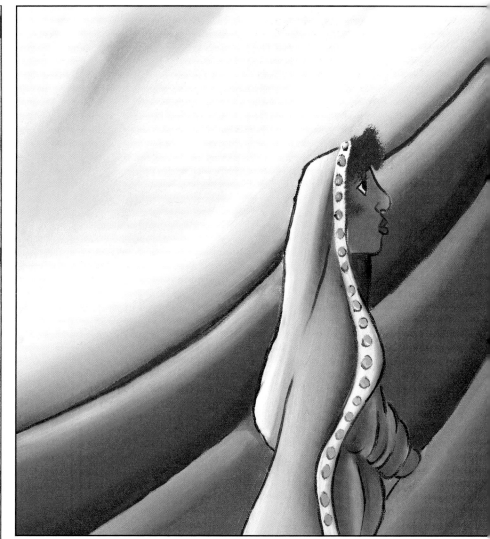

Esther

A Jewish man named Mordecai lived with his family in Persia. Mordecai had a cousin named Hadassah, who had no father or mother. So Mordecai took care of her. Hadassah was also called Esther, and she had a very pretty figure and face. When the king of Persia, King Xerxes, ordered the search for beautiful women, many girls had been brought to the palace in Susa. When this happened,

Esther was also taken to the king's palace. No one knew Esther was a Jew because Mordecai had warned her not to tell anyone.

When the king met Esther, he fell in love with her right away and crowned her queen.

Mordecai had become a palace official and found out that two men who were in charge of guarding the king had decided to kill King Xerxes. Mordecai went to Queen Esther and asked her to warn the king. When King Xerxes found out that Mordecai's story was true, he had the two men killed.

After these things happened, King Xerxes honored Haman (who was a descendant of King Agag who had fought the Jews). He gave Haman a new rank that was higher than all the important men. And all the royal officers at the king's gate would bow down and kneel before Haman. This was what the king had ordered. But Mordecai would not bow down, and he did not kneel.

Then Haman saw that Mordecai would not bow down to him or kneel before him. And he became very angry. He had been told who the people of Mordecai were. And he thought of himself as too important to try to kill only Mordecai. So he looked for a way to destroy all of Mordecai's people, the Jews, in all of Xerxes' kingdom.

Haman went to the king and suggested to him that the kingdom simply do away with all the Jewish people.

So the king took his signet ring and gave it to Haman. The king said, "The money and the people are yours. Do with them as you please."

Letters were written in the name of King Xerxes and sealed with his signet ring. They were sent by messengers to all the king's empire. The order said to kill all the Jews on a single day. That was to be the thirteenth day of the twelfth month, which was Adar. And it said to take all the things that belonged to the Jews.

Mordecai told Esther's servant to tell Esther what Haman was planning and to ask her to beg the king to have pity on her

people, the Jews.

The law said that Esther could not go to the king unless the king asked to see her. But Mordecai reminded her that if she didn't do something, she too would be put to death. "And who knows, you may have been chosen queen for just such a time as this," he said.

Esther had to do something to save her people, even if it meant her own death. So Esther dressed in her royal robes and went to see the king. He did not punish her, but was happy to see her and allowed her to come in. The king asked, "What is it, Queen Esther? What do you want to ask me? I will give you as much as half of my kingdom."

Esther did not tell the king right away why she had come to see him. Instead, she asked him to bring Haman to dinner. At dinner, the king again asked Esther what she wanted. This time Esther answered, "If it pleases you, let me live. This is what I ask. And let my people live, too. Our enemy is this wicked Haman!"

Then Haman was filled with terror before the king and queen. The king was very angry; he immediately ordered Haman killed.

Before the end of the day, the king gave Esther permission to make a law to save the lives of the Jewish people. It was a time of happiness, joy, gladness and honor for the Jews.

from **Esther 2:7—8:16**

Solomon and the Shulamite

King Solomon and the Shulamite woman were very much in love. They wanted to explain to each other and to their friends why they loved each other.

They wrote beautiful words to describe the feeling between

them. This poem is a wonderful picture of love between husband and wife. They obviously respect and care for each other in the way God meant for a husband and wife to love each other.

He said to her:

My darling, you are beautiful!

Oh, you are beautiful!

Your eyes are like doves!

Among the young women, my darling is like a lily among
    thorns!

She said:

My lover is mine, and I am his.

On their wedding day, Solomon said to his wife:

My sister, my bride, you have thrilled my heart.

You are like a garden
fountain—a well of
fresh water

flowing down from the
mountains of
Lebanon.

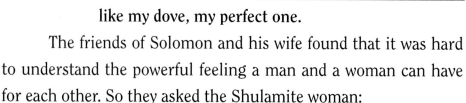

There may be 60 queens
and 80 slave women

and so many girls you
cannot count them.

But there is only one
like my dove, my perfect one.

The friends of Solomon and his wife found that it was hard to understand the powerful feeling a man and a woman can have for each other. So they asked the Shulamite woman:

Is your lover better than other lovers,
you, the most beautiful of women?

She tried to explain all the reasons that they could see:

My lover is clean and tanned.

He's the best of 10,000 men.

His head is like the finest gold.

His hair is wavy and black like a raven.

His legs are like large marble posts,
standing on bases of fine gold.

Solomon spoke of her, saying:

Love is as strong as death.

Desire is as strong as the grave.

Love bursts into flames.

It burns like a very hot fire.

Even much water cannot put out the flame of love.

Floods cannot drown love.

If a man offered everything in his house for love,

people would totally reject it.

And in the end, she explained that most of all, he was her friend.

from Song of Solomon 1—8

Ebed-Melech

Jeremiah was a great prophet of God. He lived in Jerusalem and gave the people the messages that God had told him to give them.

When Jeremiah told them that the city would soon be defeated by their enemies, the people didn't like to hear what God had to say. They put Jeremiah in prison.

The king of Israel, King Zedekiah, liked Jeremiah, but he gave in to his officials, who didn't just want Jeremiah in prison—they wanted him to die! Four of them went to the king and said, "Jeremiah must be put to death! He is discouraging everyone by the things he is saying. He does not want good to happen to us. He wants to ruin the people of Jerusalem."

King Zedekiah said to them, "Jeremiah is in your control. I cannot do anything to stop you!"

The four men took Jeremiah and used ropes to let him

down into a well that belonged to the king's son. It did not have any water in it, only mud. And Jeremiah sank down in the mud.

But Ebed-Melech heard that the officers had put Jeremiah into the well. Ebed-Melech was a Cushite (from Ethiopia), and he was a eunuch in the palace. King Zedekiah was sitting at the Benjamin Gate. So Ebed-Melech left the palace and went to the king. Ebed-Melech said, "My master and king, the rulers have treated Jeremiah the prophet badly! They have thrown him into a well! They have left him there to die! When there is no more bread in the city, he will starve."

Then King Zedekiah commanded Ebed-Melech the Cushite: "Ebed-Melech, take 30 men from the palace with you. Go and lift Jeremiah the prophet out of the well before he dies."

So Ebed-Melech took the men with him. And he went to a room under the storeroom in the palace. He took some old rags and worn-out clothes from that room. Then he let those rags down with some ropes to Jeremiah in the well. Ebed-Melech the Cushite said to Jeremiah, "Put these old rags and worn-out clothes under your arms. They will be pads for the ropes." So Jeremiah did as Ebed-Melech said. The men pulled Jeremiah up with the ropes and lifted him out of the well. And Jeremiah stayed under guard in the courtyard.

Later, while Jeremiah was a prisoner in the courtyard of the palace guards, the Lord told him to say to Ebed-Melech the

Cushite:

"Very soon I will make my words about Jerusalem come true. They will come through disaster, not through good times. You will see everything come true with your own eyes. But I will save you on that day, Ebed-Melech, says the Lord. You will not be handed over to the people you fear. I will surely save you, Ebed-Melech. You will not die from a sword. But you will escape and live. This will happen because you have trusted in me."

God takes care of those who love and obey him.

from **Jeremiah 38:4–13; 39:15–18**

Shadrach, Meshach and Abednego

Now King Nebuchadnezzar had a gold statue made. That statue was 90 feet high and 9 feet wide. He commanded that the people of every nation and race bow down and worship the statue. Anyone who refused would at once be thrown into a flam-

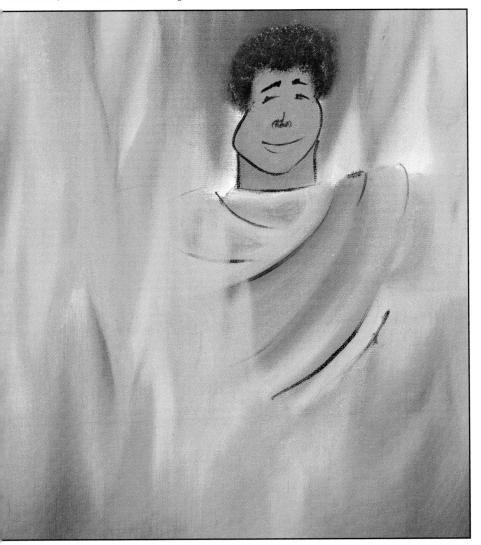

ing furnace. Everyone did as the king ordered, except for three men: Shadrach, Meshach and Abednego.

Nebuchadnezzar became very angry. He called for Shadrach, Meshach and Abednego. So those men were brought to the king. And Nebuchadnezzar said, "Shadrach, Meshach and Abednego, is it true that you do not serve my gods? And is it true that you did not worship the gold statue I have set up? Now, you will hear the sound of the horns, flutes, lyres, zithers, harps, pipes and all the other musical instruments. And you must be ready to bow down and worship the statue I made. That will be good. But if you do not worship it, you will be thrown quickly into the blazing furnace. Then no god will be able to save you from my power."

Shadrach, Meshach and Abednego answered the king. They said, "Nebuchadnezzar, we do not need to defend ourselves to you. You can throw us into the blazing furnace. The God we serve is able to save us from the furnace and your power. If he does this, it is good. But even if God does not save us, we want you, our king, to know this: We will not serve your gods. We will not worship the gold statue you have set up."

Then Nebuchadnezzar was furious with Shadrach, Meshach and Abednego. He ordered the furnace to be heated seven times hotter than usual. Then he commanded some of the strongest soldiers in his army to tie up Shadrach, Meshach and Abednego. The king told the soldiers to throw them into the blazing furnace.

So Shadrach, Meshach and Abednego were tied up and thrown into the blazing furnace. They were still wearing their robes, trousers, turbans and other clothes. The king was very angry when he gave the command. And the furnace was made very hot. The fire was so hot that the flames killed the strong soldiers who took Shadrach, Meshach and Abednego there. Firmly tied, Shadrach, Meshach and Abednego fell into the blazing furnace.

Then King Nebuchadnezzar was very surprised and jumped to his feet. He asked the men who advised him, "Didn't we tie up only three men? Didn't we throw them into the fire?"

They answered, "Yes, our king."

The king said, "Look! I see four men. They are walking around in the fire. They are not tied up, and they are not burned. The fourth man looks like a son of the gods."

Then Nebuchadnezzar went to the opening of the blazing furnace. He shouted, "Shadrach, Meshach and Abednego, come out! Servants of the Most High God, come here!"

So Shadrach, Meshach and Abednego came out of the fire. When they came out, the princes, assistant governors, governors and royal advisers crowded around them. They saw that the fire had not harmed their bodies. Their hair was not burned. Their robes were not burned. And they didn't even smell like smoke.

Then Nebuchadnezzar said, "Praise the God of Shadrach, Meshach and Abednego. Their God has sent his angel and saved his servants from the fire!

from **Daniel 3:1–3, 12–30**

Daniel
and the Lions' Den

Darius the Mede took over the kingdom of Babylon after King Belshazzar had been killed. Darius let Daniel govern the whole kingdom. Of course, this did not go over well with the other officials. So the other supervisors and the governors tried to find

reasons to accuse Daniel. But he went on doing the business of the government. And they could not find anything wrong with him. So they could not accuse him of doing anything wrong. Daniel was trustworthy. He was not lazy and did not cheat the king. Finally these men said, "We will never find any reason to accuse Daniel. But we must find something to complain about. It will have to be about the law of his God."

So the supervisors and the governors went as a group to the king. They said: "We think the king should make this law that everyone would have to obey: No one should pray to any god or man except to you, our king. This should be done for the next 30 days. Anyone who doesn't obey will be thrown into the lions' den. Now, our king, make the law. Write it down so it cannot be changed." So King Darius made the law and had it written.

When Daniel heard that the new law had been written, he went to his house. He went to his upstairs room. The windows of that room opened toward Jerusalem. Three times each day Daniel got down on his knees and prayed. He prayed and thanked God, just as he always had done.

Then those men went as a group and found Daniel. They saw him praying and asking God for help. So they went to the king. They talked to him about the law he had made. They said, "Didn't you write a law that says no one may pray to any god or man except you, our king? Doesn't it say that anyone who disobeys during the next 30 days will be thrown into the lions' den?"

The king answered, "Yes, I wrote that law." The men told the king that Daniel refused to obey his law.

Darius had no choice but to order that Daniel be thrown into the pit of lions. The king said to Daniel, "May the God you serve all the time save you!" A big stone was brought. It was put over the opening of the lions' den. Then the king used his signet ring to put his special seal on the rock. And he used the rings of his royal officers to put their seals on the rock also. This showed that no one could move that rock and bring Daniel out. Then

King Darius went back to his palace. He did not eat that night. He did not have any entertainment brought to entertain him. And he could not sleep.

The next morning King Darius got up at dawn. He hurried to the lions' den. As he came near the den, he was worried. He called out to Daniel. He said, "Daniel, servant of the living God! Has your God that you always worship been able to save you from the lions?"

Daniel answered, "My king, live forever! My God sent his angel to close the lions' mouths. They have not hurt me, because my God knows I am innocent. I never did anything wrong to you, my king."

King Darius was very happy. He told his servants to lift Daniel out of the lions' den. So they lifted him out and did not find any injury on him. This was because Daniel had trusted in his God.

Then the king gave a command. The men who had accused Daniel were brought to the lions' den and thrown into it.

Then King Darius wrote a letter. It was to all people and all nations, to those who spoke every language in the world: "I am making a new law. This law is for people in every part of my kingdom. All of you must fear and respect the God of Daniel. Daniel's God is the living God. He lives forever. His kingdom will never be destroyed. His rule will never end."

from **Daniel 5:30—6:26**

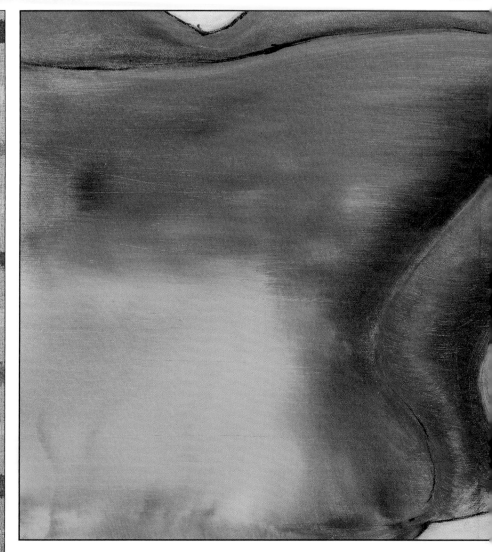

Jonah

The Lord spoke his word to Jonah son of Amittai: "Get up, go to the great city of Nineveh and preach against it. I see the evil things they do."

But Jonah got up to run away from the Lord. He went to the city of Joppa. There he found a ship that was going to the city

of Tarshish. Jonah paid for the trip and went aboard. He wanted to go to Tarshish to run away from the Lord.

But the Lord sent a great wind on the sea. This wind made the sea very rough. So the ship was in danger of breaking apart. The sailors were afraid. Each man cried to his own god.

They said to Jonah, "Tell us what you have done. Why has this terrible thing happened to us?"

Then Jonah said to them, "I am a Hebrew. I fear the Lord, the God of heaven. He is the God who made the sea and the land."

Then the men were very afraid. They asked Jonah, "What terrible thing did you do?" They knew Jonah was running away from the Lord.

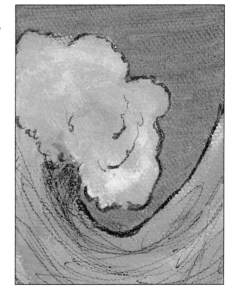

The wind and the waves of the sea were becoming much stronger. So the men said to Jonah, "What should we do to you to make the sea calm down?"

Jonah said to them, "Pick me up, and throw me into the sea. Then it will calm down. I know it is my fault that this great storm has come on you."

Instead, the men tried to row the ship back to the land. But they could not. The wind and the waves of the sea were becoming much stronger.

So the men cried to the Lord, "Lord, please don't let us die because of taking this man's life. Please don't think we are guilty of killing an innocent man. Lord, you have caused all of this to happen. You wanted it this way." Then the men picked up Jonah and threw him into the sea. So the sea became calm.

And the Lord caused a very big fish to swallow Jonah. Jonah was in the stomach of the fish three days and three nights.

Jonah was really in a bad situation. In the belly of a fish, at the bottom of the sea, Jonah prayed to the Lord and promised to do what the Lord told him to do. The Lord heard Jonah's prayers and commanded the fish to throw up Jonah onto the shore.

Then the Lord spoke his word to Jonah again. The Lord

said, "Get up. Go to the great city of Nineveh. Preach against it what I tell you." This time Jonah obeyed the Lord. He went to Nineveh and warned the people of the Lord's plan to destroy their city.

When the king of Nineveh heard this news . . . he made an announcement and sent it through the city. The announcement said: "No person or animal should eat anything. . . . People should cry loudly to God. Everyone must turn away from his evil life. Everyone must stop doing harm. Maybe God will change his mind. Maybe he will stop being angry. Then we will not die."

God saw what the people did. He saw that they stopped doing evil things. So God changed his mind and did not do what he had warned. He did not punish them.

from **Jonah 1:1—3:10**

Mary and Elizabeth

An angel of the Lord, Gabriel, appeared to Mary and Elizabeth to tell them that they would give birth to very special babies.

First, the angel told Elizabeth, who was very old and long past the age of having babies, that she and her husband Zechariah would be blessed with a son, who would come to be known as John

the Baptist. He would be a great servant of the Lord and would lead many people to salvation through the Lord, Jesus Christ.

During Elizabeth's sixth month of pregnancy, God sent the angel Gabriel to a virgin who lived in Nazareth, a town in Galilee. She was engaged to marry a man named Joseph from the family of David. Her name was Mary. The angel came to her and said, "Greetings! The Lord has blessed you and is with you."

But Mary was very confused by what the angel said. Mary wondered, "What does this mean?"

The angel said to her, "Don't be afraid, Mary, because God is pleased with you. Listen! You will become pregnant. You will give birth to a son, and you will name him Jesus. He will be great, and people will call him the Son of the Most High. The Lord God will give him the throne of King David, his ancestor. He will rule over the people of Jacob forever. His kingdom will never end."

Mary said to the angel, "How will this happen? I am a virgin!"

The angel said to Mary, "The Holy Spirit will come upon you, and the power of the Most High will cover you. The baby will be holy. He will be called the Son of God. Now listen! Elizabeth, your relative, is very old. But she is also pregnant with a son. Everyone thought she could not have a baby, but she has been pregnant for six months. God can do everything!"

Mary said, "I am the servant girl of the Lord. Let this happen to me as you say!" Then the angel went away.

Mary got up and went quickly to a town in the mountains of Judea. She went to Zechariah's house and greeted Elizabeth. When Elizabeth heard Mary's greeting, the unborn baby inside Elizabeth jumped. Then Elizabeth was filled with the Holy Spirit. She cried out in a loud voice, "God has blessed you more than any other woman. And God has blessed the baby which you will give birth to. You are the mother of my Lord, and you have come to me! Why has something so good happened to me? When I heard your voice, the baby inside me jumped with joy. You are blessed because you believed what the Lord said to you would really happen."

Then Mary said, "My soul praises the Lord; my heart is happy because God is my Savior. I am not important, but God has shown his care for me, his servant girl. From now on, all people will say that I am blessed, because the Powerful One has done great things for me. His name is holy. God will always give mercy to those who worship him."

from **Luke 1:11–50**

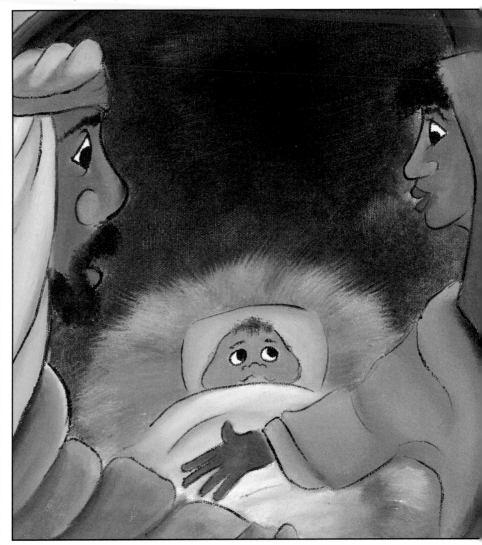

The Birth of Jesus

At that time, Augustus Caesar sent an order to all people in the countries that were under Roman rule. The order said that they must list their names in a register. And everyone went to their own towns to be registered.

So Joseph left Nazareth, a town in Galilee. He went to the town of Bethlehem in Judea. This town was known as the town of

David. Joseph went there because he was from the family of David. Joseph registered with Mary because she was engaged to marry him. (Mary was now pregnant.) While Joseph and Mary were in Bethlehem, the time came for her to have the baby. She gave birth to her first son. There were no rooms left in the inn. So she wrapped the baby with cloths and laid him in a box where animals are fed.

That night, some shepherds were in the fields nearby watching their sheep. An angel of the Lord stood before them. The glory of the Lord was shining around them, and suddenly they became very frightened. The angel said to them, "Don't be afraid, because I am bringing you some good news. It will be a joy to all the people. Today your Savior was born in David's town. He is Christ, the Lord. This is how you will know him: You will find a baby wrapped in cloths and lying in a feeding box."

Then a very large group of angels from heaven joined the first angel. All the angels were praising God, saying: "Give glory to God in heaven, and on earth let there be peace to the people who please God."

After Jesus was born, some wise men from the east came to Jerusalem. They asked, "Where is the baby who was born to be the king of the Jews? We saw his star in the east. We came to worship him."

When King Herod heard about this new king of the Jews, he was troubled. And all the people in Jerusalem were worried too. Herod called a meeting of all the leading priests and teachers of the law. He asked them where the Christ would be born. They answered, "In the town of Bethlehem in Judea. The prophet wrote about this in the Scriptures."

Then Herod had a secret meeting with the wise men from the east. He learned from them the exact time they first saw the star. Then Herod sent the wise men to Bethlehem. He said to them, "Go and look carefully to find the child. When you find him, come tell me. Then I can go worship him too."

The wise men heard the king and then left. They saw the same star they had seen in the east. It went before them until it stopped above the place where the child was. When the wise men saw the star, they were filled with joy. They went to the house where the child was and saw him with his mother, Mary. They bowed down and worshiped the child. They opened the gifts they brought for him. They gave him treasures of gold, frankincense, and myrrh. But God warned the wise men in a dream not to go back to Herod. So they went home to their own country by a different way.

from Matthew 2:1b–5, 7–15; Luke 2:1, 3–14

Jesus Grows Up

After the wise men left, an angel of the Lord came to Joseph in a dream. The angel said, "Get up! Take the child and his mother and escape to Egypt. Herod will start looking for the child to kill him. Stay in Egypt until I tell you to return."

So Joseph got up and left for Egypt during the night with the child and his mother. Joseph stayed in Egypt until Herod died.

This was to make clear the full meaning of what the Lord had said through the prophet. The Lord said, "I called my son out of Egypt."[n]

After Herod died, an angel of the Lord came to Joseph in a dream. This happened while Joseph was in Egypt. The angel said, "Get up! Take the child and his mother and go to Israel. The people who were trying to kill the child are now dead."

So Joseph got up and left with them for Israel. But he heard that Archelaus was now king in Judea. Archelaus became king when his father Herod died. So Joseph was afraid to go there. After being warned in a dream, he went to the area of Galilee. He went to a town called Nazareth and lived there.

The little child began to grow up. He became stronger and wiser, and God's bless-ings were with him.

Every year Jesus' parents went to Jerusalem for the Passover Feast. When Jesus was 12 years old, they went to the feast as they always did. When the feast days were over, they went home. The boy Jesus stayed behind in Jerusalem, but his parents did not know it. Joseph and Mary traveled for a whole day. They thought that Jesus was with them in the group. Then they began to look for him among their family and friends, but they did not find him. So they went back to Jerusalem to look for him there. After three days they found him. Jesus was sitting in the Temple with the religious teachers, listening to them and asking them questions. All who heard him were amazed at his understanding and wise answers. When Jesus' parents saw him, they were amazed. His mother said to him, "Son, why did you do this to us? Your father and I were very worried about you. We have been looking for you."

Jesus asked, "Why did you have to look for me? You should have known that I must be where my Father's work is!" But they did not understand the meaning of what he said.

Jesus went with them to Nazareth and obeyed them. His mother was still thinking about all that had happened. Jesus continued to learn more and more and to grow physically. People liked him, and he pleased God.

from Matthew 2:13–15, 19–23; Luke 2:40–52

[n]"I called . . . Egypt." Quotation from Hosea 11:1.

John the Baptist

John the Baptist came and began preaching in the desert area of Judea. John said, "Change your hearts and lives because the kingdom of heaven is coming soon."

John's clothes were made from camel's hair. He wore a leather belt around his waist. For food, he ate locusts and wild honey. Many people went to hear John preach. They came from

Jerusalem and all Judea and all the area around the Jordan River. They told of the sins they had done, and John baptized them in the Jordan River.

Many of the Pharisees and Sadducees came to the place where John was baptizing people. When John saw them, he said: "You are all snakes! Who warned you to run away from God's anger that is coming? You must do something to show that you have really changed your hearts and lives."

The people asked John, "What should we do?"

John answered, "If you have two shirts, share with the person who does not have one. If you have food, share that too."

Even tax collectors came to John to be baptized. They said to John, "Teacher, what should we do?"

John said to them, "Don't take more taxes from people than you have been ordered to take."

The soldiers asked John, "What about us? What should we do?"

John said to them, "Don't force people to give you money. Don't lie about them. Be satisfied with the pay you get."

All the people were hoping for the Christ to come, and they wondered about John. They thought, "Maybe he is the Christ."

John answered everyone, "I baptize you with water, but there is one coming later who can do more than I can. I am not good enough to untie his sandals. He will baptize you with the Holy Spirit and with fire." And John continued to preach the Good News, saying many other things to encourage the people.

At that time Jesus came from Galilee to the Jordan River. He came to John and wanted John to baptize him. But John tried to stop him. John said, "Why do you come to me to be baptized? I should be baptized by you!"

Jesus answered, "Let it be this way for now. We should do all things that are right." So John agreed to baptize Jesus.

Jesus was baptized and came up out of the water. Heaven opened, and he saw God's Spirit coming down on him like a dove.

And a voice spoke from heaven. The voice said, "This is my Son and I love him. I am very pleased with him."

from **Matthew 3:1, 2, 4–8, 13–17; Luke 3:10–16, 18**

Water to Wine

There was a wedding in the town of Cana in Galilee. Jesus' mother was there. Jesus and his followers were also invited to the wedding.

A wedding during the time of Jesus often lasted several days, with lots of parties. It was very important that the guests have enough food and wine. But halfway through this wedding, they ran out of wine. Mary knew that the people would be embarrassed. When the wine was gone, Jesus' mother said to him, "They have no more wine."

Jesus answered, "Dear woman, why come to me? My time has not yet come."

His mother said to the servants, "Do whatever he tells you to do." She knew that Jesus would do the right thing and help out the people at the wedding.

In that place there were six stone water jars. The Jews used jars like these in their washing ceremony.[n] Each jar held about 20 or 30 gallons.

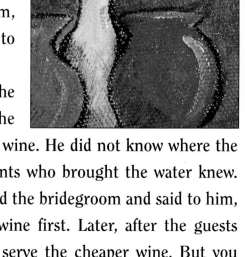

Jesus said to the servants, "Fill the jars with water." So they filled the jars to the top.

Then he said to them, "Now take some out and give it to the master of the feast.

So the servants took the water to the master. When he tasted it, the water had become wine. He did not know where the wine came from. But the servants who brought the water knew. The master of the wedding called the bridegroom and said to him, "People always serve the best wine first. Later, after the guests have been drinking a lot, they serve the cheaper wine. But you have saved the best wine till now."

So in Cana of Galilee, Jesus did his first miracle. There he showed his glory, and his followers believed in him.

Then Jesus went to the town of Capernaum with his mother, brothers and his followers. They all stayed in Capernaum for a few days. Sometimes we think that sad times are the only times people think about God, but Jesus did this miracle—his first—at a party! Jesus enjoyed happy gatherings of people. He didn't preach at the wedding, but he added to the joy there by supplying more wine. He did some very serious work later when he preached and taught and healed people. But Jesus knew that happy times are also good times to think about him.

from **John 2:1-12**

[n]washing ceremony The Jews washed themselves in special ways before eating, before worshiping in the Temple, and at other special times.

Jesus' Disciples

One day Jesus was standing beside Lake Galilee. Many people were pressing all around him. They wanted to hear the word of God. Jesus saw two boats at the shore of the lake. The fishermen had left them and were washing their nets. Jesus got into one of the boats, the one which belonged to Simon.[n] Jesus asked Si-

mon to push off a little from the land. Then Jesus sat down in the boat and continued to teach the people on the shore.

When Jesus had finished speaking, he said to Simon, "Take the boat into deep water. If you will put your nets in the water, you will catch some fish."

Simon answered, "Master, we worked hard all night trying to catch fish, but we caught nothing. But you say to put the nets in the water; so I will." The fishermen did as Jesus told them. And they caught so many fish that the nets began to break. They called

139

to their friends in the other boat to come and help them. The friends came, and both boats were filled so full that they were almost sinking.

When Simon Peter saw what had happened, he bowed down before Jesus and said, "Go away from me, Lord. I am a sinful man!"

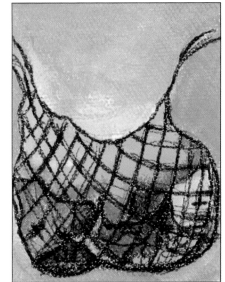

Jesus said to Simon, "Don't be afraid. From now on you will be fishermen for men." When the men brought their boats to the shore, they left everything and followed Jesus.

Jesus saw James and John, the sons of Zebedee. They were in a boat with their father Zebedee, preparing their nets to catch fish. Jesus told them to come with him. At once they left the boat and their father, and they followed Jesus.

Later, Jesus saw a man named Matthew. Matthew was sitting in the tax office. Jesus said to him, "Follow me." And Matthew stood up and followed Jesus.

Jesus had dinner at Matthew's house. Many tax collectors and "sinners" came and ate with Jesus and his followers. The Pharisees saw this and asked Jesus' followers, "Why does your teacher eat with tax collectors and 'sinners'?"

Jesus heard the Pharisees ask this. So he said, "Healthy people don't need a doctor. Only the sick need a doctor. Go and learn what this means: 'I want faithful love more than I want animal sacrifices.'[n] I did not come to invite good people. I came to invite sinners."

Then Jesus went up on a hill and called some men to come to him. These were the men Jesus wanted, and they went up to him. Jesus chose 12 men and called them apostles. He wanted these 12 to be with him, and he wanted to send them to other places to preach. He also wanted them to have the power to force demons out of people. These are the 12 men he chose: Simon (Jesus gave him the name Peter), James and John, the sons of Zebedee (they talked so much and so loudly that Jesus gave them a nickname that meant "Thunderbolts"), Andrew, Philip, Bartholomew, Matthew, Thomas, James the son of Alphaeus, Thaddaeus, Simon the Zealot, and Judas Iscariot. Judas is the one who gave Jesus to his enemies.

from Matthew 4:21, 22; 9:9–13; Mark 3:13–19; Luke 5:1–11

[n]Simon Simon's other name was Peter.
[n]'I want . . . sacrifices.' Quotation from Hosea 6:6.

Jesus Feeds
Five Thousand

Jesus had sent the apostles out to teach people about God. When they returned, they gathered around him and told him about all the things they had done and taught. Crowds of people were coming and going. Jesus and his followers did not even have time

to eat. He said to them, "Come with me. We will go to a quiet place to be alone. There we will get some rest."

So they went in a boat alone to a place where there were no people. But many people saw them leave and recognized them. So people from all the towns ran to the place where Jesus was going. They got there before Jesus arrived. When he landed, he saw a great crowd waiting. Jesus felt sorry for them, because they were like sheep without a shepherd. So he taught them many things.

143

It was now late in the day. Jesus' followers came to him and said, "No one lives in this place. And it is already very late. Send the people away. They need to go to the farms and towns around here to buy some food to eat."

But Jesus answered, "You give them food to eat."

They said to him, "We can't buy enough bread to feed all these people! We would all have to work a month to earn enough money to buy that much bread!"

Jesus asked them, "How many loaves of bread do you have now? Go and see."

Another follower there was Andrew. He was Simon Peter's brother. Andrew said, "Here is a boy with five loaves of barley bread and two little fish. But that is not enough for so many people."

Then Jesus said to the followers, "Tell all the people to sit in groups on the green grass." So all the people sat in groups of 50 or groups of 100. Jesus took the five loaves and two fish. He looked up to heaven and thanked God for the bread. He divided the bread and gave it to his followers for them to give to the people. Then he divided the two fish among them all. All the people ate and were satisfied. The followers filled 12 baskets with the pieces of bread and fish that were not eaten.

There were about 5,000 men there who ate, as well as women and children.

The people saw this miracle that Jesus did. They said, "He must truly be the Prophet[n] who is coming into the world."

Jesus knew that the people planned to come and take him by force and make him their king. So he left and went into the hills alone.

from Matthew 14:21; Mark 6:30–43; John 6:8, 9, 14, 15

[n]**Prophet** They probably meant the prophet that God told Moses he would send (Deuteronomy 18:15–19).

Sermon
on the Mount

Thousands came to hear Jesus' Sermon on the Mount. **Jesus** saw the crowds who were there. He went up on a hill and sat down. His followers came to him. Jesus taught the people. This is

what Jesus said:

"Those people who know they have great spiritual needs are happy. The kingdom of heaven belongs to them.

"Those who are sad now are happy. God will comfort them.

"Those who are humble are happy. The earth will belong to them.

"Those who want to do right more than anything else are happy. God will fully satisfy them.

"Those who give mercy to others are happy. Mercy will be given to them.

"Those who are pure in their thinking are happy. They will be with God.

"Those who work to bring peace are happy. God will call them his sons.

"Those who are treated badly for doing good are happy. The kingdom of heaven belongs to them.

"People will say bad things about you and hurt you. They will lie and say all kinds of evil things about you because you follow me. But when they do these things to you, you are happy. Rejoice and be glad. You have a great reward waiting for you in heaven. People did the same evil things to the prophets who lived before you.

"You are the salt of the earth. But if the salt loses its salty taste, it cannot be made salty again. It is good for nothing. It must be thrown out for people to walk on.

"You are the light that gives light to the world. A city that is built on a hill cannot be hidden. And people don't hide a light under a bowl. They put the light on a lampstand. Then the light shines for all the people in the house. In the same way, you should be a light for other people. Live so that they will see the good things you do. Live so that they will praise your Father in heaven."

from Matthew 5:1-16

Stories Jesus Told

At the end of his Sermon on the Mount, Jesus suggested that everyone take a good look at their lives and try to live according to God's law. He told several stories that showed people how to live.

Jesus said: "Be careful! When you do good things, don't do

them in front of people to be seen by them. If you do that, then you will have no reward from your Father in heaven.

"When you give to the poor, don't be like the hypocrites. They blow trumpets before they give so that people will see them. They do that in the synagogues and on the streets. They want other people to honor them. I tell you the truth. Those hypocrites already have their full reward. So when you give to the poor, give very secretly. Don't let anyone know what you are doing. Your giving should be done in secret. Your Father can see what is done in secret, and he will reward you.

"Don't judge other people, and you will not be judged. Don't accuse others of being guilty, and you will not be accused of being guilty. Forgive other people, and you will be forgiven. Give, and you will receive. You will be given much. It will be poured into your hands—more than you can hold. You will be given so much that it will spill into your lap. The way you give to others is the way God will give to you.

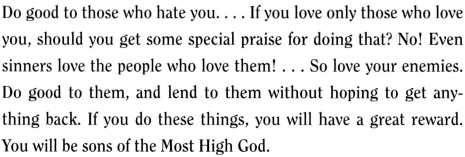

"I say to you who are listening to me, love your enemies. Do good to those who hate you. . . . If you love only those who love you, should you get some special praise for doing that? No! Even sinners love the people who love them! . . . So love your enemies. Do good to them, and lend to them without hoping to get anything back. If you do these things, you will have a great reward. You will be sons of the Most High God.

"Everyone who hears these things I say and obeys them is like a wise man. The wise man built his house on rock. It rained hard and the water rose. The winds blew and hit that house. But the house did not fall, because the house was built on rock. But the person who hears the things I teach and does not obey them is like a foolish man. The foolish man built his house on sand. It rained hard, the water rose, and the winds blew and hit that house. And the house fell with a big crash."

When Jesus finished saying these things, the people were

amazed at his teaching. Jesus did not teach like their teachers of the law. He taught like a person who had authority. All who heard had a choice to make.

from **Matthew 6:1–4; 7:24–29; Luke 6:27, 32, 35, 37, 38**

The Mustard Seed

Another time Jesus began teaching by the lake. A great crowd gathered around him. So he got into a boat and went out on the lake. All the people stayed on the shore close to the water. Jesus used many stories to teach them. He said, "Listen! A farmer went out to plant his seed. While the farmer was planting, some seed fell by the road. The birds came and ate all that seed. Some

seed fell on rocky ground where there wasn't much dirt. The seed grew very fast there because the ground was not deep. But when the sun rose, the plants withered. The plants died because they did not have deep roots. Some other seed fell among thorny weeds. The weeds grew and choked the good plants. So those plants did not make grain. Some other seed fell on good ground. In the good ground, the seed began to grow. It grew and made a crop of grain. Some plants made 30 times more grain, some 60 times more grain, and some 100 times more grain."

Then Jesus said, "You people who hear me, listen!"

Later, when Jesus was alone, the 12 apostles and others around him asked him about the stories.

Jesus said, "Only you can know the secret truth about the kingdom of God. But to other people I tell everything by using stories. I do this so that: 'They will look and look, but they will not learn. They will listen and listen, but they will not understand. If they did learn and understand, they would come back to me and be forgiven.'"

Then Jesus said to the followers, "Do you understand this story? If you don't, then how will you understand any story? The farmer is like a person who plants God's teaching in people. Sometimes the teaching falls on the road. This is like some people. They hear the teaching of God. But Satan quickly comes and takes away the teaching that was planted in them. Others are like the seed planted on rocky ground. They hear the teaching and quickly accept it with joy. But they don't allow the teaching to go deep into their lives. They keep it only a short time. When trouble or persecution comes because of the teaching, they quickly give up. Others are like the seed planted among the thorny weeds. They hear the teaching. But then other things come into their lives: worries, the love of money, and wanting all kinds of other things. These things stop the teaching from growing. So that teaching does not produce fruit[n] in their lives. Others are like the seed planted in the good ground. They hear the teaching and accept it.

Then they grow and produce fruit—sometimes 30 times more, sometimes 60 times more, and sometimes 100 times more."

Then Jesus said, "How can I show you what the kingdom of God is like? What story can I use to explain it? The kingdom of God is like a mustard seed. The mustard seed is the smallest seed you plant in the ground. But when you plant this seed, it grows and becomes the largest of all garden plants. It produces large branches. Even the wild birds can make nests in it and be protected from the sun."

Jesus used many stories like these to teach them. He taught them all that they could understand. He always used stories to teach them. But when he and his followers were alone together, Jesus explained everything to them.

from **Mark 4:1–20, 30–34**

[n]produce fruit To produce fruit means to have in your life the good things God wants.   *157*

Jesus Walks on the Water

After Jesus had fed the five thousand, his disciples got into a boat to cross over the lake to Bethsaida. **Jesus stayed there to tell the people they could go home.** Then he told them goodbye and went up on the side of a mountain to pray.

Later that same evening, Jesus was still on the mountain

alone. By this time, the boat was already far away somewhere in the middle of the lake. The boat was having trouble because of the waves, and the wind was blowing against it. The disciples were struggling very hard to keep control of the boat against the strong winds.

Between three and six o'clock in the morning, Jesus' followers were still in the boat. Jesus came to them. He was walking on the water. When the followers saw him walking on the water, they were afraid. They said, "It's a ghost!" and cried out in fear.

159

But Jesus quickly spoke to them. He said, "Have courage! It is I! Don't be afraid."

Peter said, "Lord, if that is really you, then tell me to come to you on the water."

Jesus said, "Come."

And Peter left the boat and walked on the water to Jesus. But when Peter saw the wind and the waves he became afraid and began to sink. He shouted, "Lord, save me!"

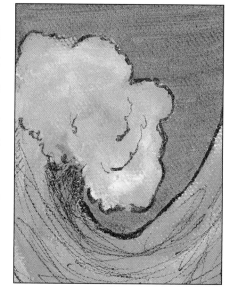

Then Jesus reached out his hand and caught Peter. Jesus said, "Your faith is small. Why did you doubt?"

After Peter and Jesus were in the boat, the wind became calm. Then those who were in the boat worshiped Jesus and said, "Truly you are the Son of God!"

After they crossed the lake, they came to the shore at Gennesaret. As soon as they got out of the boat, the people recognized Jesus.

The next day came. Some people had stayed on the other side of the lake. They knew that Jesus had not gone in the boat with his followers but that they had left without him. And they knew that only one boat had been there. But then some boats came from Tiberias. They landed near the place where the people had eaten the bread after the Lord had given thanks. The people saw that Jesus and his followers were not there now. So they got into their boats and went to Capernaum. They wanted to find

Jesus.

The people found Jesus on the other side of the lake. They asked him, "Teacher, when did you come here?"

Jesus answered, "Are you looking for me because you saw me do miracles? No! I tell you the truth. You are looking for me because you ate the bread and were satisfied. Earthly food spoils and ruins. So don't work to get that kind of food. But work to get the food that stays good always and gives you eternal life. The Son of Man will give you that food. God the Father has shown that he is with the Son of Man."

The people said, "Sir, give us this bread always."

Then Jesus said, "I am the bread that gives life. He who comes to me will never be hungry. He who believes in me will never be thirsty. But as I told you before, you have seen me, and still you don't believe. The Father gives me my people. Every one of them will come to me and I will always accept them."

But the people still came to Jesus, not to believe in him as the Son of God, but so that he could heal them and perform other miracles. So they ran all over that part of the country to bring their sick people to him. They brought them each time they heard where he was. In every village or farm or marketplace where Jesus went, the people brought their sick to him. They begged him to let them just touch his clothes, and everyone who did was healed.

from Matthew 14:22–36; John 6:22–27, 34–37

The Good Samaritan

When Jesus spoke to his disciples, he tried to explain to them how special they were to be able to be with Jesus and hear his teachings. Many people, even those who had studied the Scriptures for a long time, could not understand what Jesus was talking about. Instead, Jesus wanted to make sure that ordinary people could hear and understand his messages.

Then the Holy Spirit made Jesus rejoice. He said, "I thank you, Father, Lord of heaven and earth, because you have hidden these things from the people who are wise and smart. But you have shown them to those who are like little children. Yes, Father, you did this because this is what you really wanted.

"My Father has given me all things. No one knows the Son—only the Father knows. And only the Son knows the Father. The only people who will know about the Father are those whom the son chooses to tell."

Then Jesus turned to his followers and said privately, "You are blessed to see what you now see! I tell you, many prophets and kings wanted to see what you now see. But they did not see these things. And many prophets and kings wanted to hear what you now hear. But they did not hear these things."

Then a teacher of the law stood up. He was trying to test Jesus. He said, "Teacher, what must I do to get life forever?"

Jesus said to him, "What is written in the law? What do you read there?"

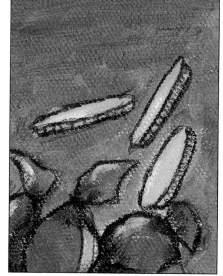

The man answered, "Love the Lord your God. Love him with all your heart, all your soul, all your strength, and all your mind."[n] Also, "You must love your neighbor as you love yourself."[n]

Jesus said to him, "Your answer is right. Do this and you will have life forever."

But the man wanted to show that the way he was living was right. So he said to Jesus, "And who is my neighbor?"

To answer this question, Jesus said, "A man was going down the road from Jerusalem to Jericho. Some robbers attacked him. They tore off his clothes and beat him. Then they left him lying there, almost dead. It happened that a Jewish priest was going down that road. When the priest saw the man, he walked by on the other side of the road. Next, a Levite[n] came there. He went over and looked at the man. Then he walked by on the other side of the road. Then a Samaritan[n] traveling down the road came to where the hurt man was lying. He saw the man and felt very sorry for him. The Samaritan went to him and poured olive oil and wine[n] on his wounds and bandaged them. He put the hurt man on his own donkey and took him to an inn. At the inn, the Samaritan took care of him. The next day, the Samaritan brought out two silver coins[n] and gave them to the innkeeper. The Samaritan said, 'Take care of this man. If you spend more money on him, I will pay it back to you when I come again.'"

Then Jesus said, "Which one of these three men do you think was a neighbor to the man who was attacked by the robbers?"

The teacher of the law answered, "The one who helped him."

Jesus said to him, "Then go and do the same thing he did."

from Luke 10:21–37

[n]"Love . . . mind." Quotation from Deuteronomy 6:5.
[n]"You . . . yourself." Quotation from Leviticus 19:18.
[n]Levite Levites were men from the tribe of Levi who helped the Jewish priests with their work in the temple. Read 1 Chronicles 23:24–32.
[n]Samaritan Samaritans were people from Samaria. These people were part Jewish, but the Jews did not accept them as true Jews. Samaritans and Jews hated each other.
[n]olive oil and wine Oil and wine were used like medicine to soften and clean wounds.
[n]silver coins A Roman denarius. One coin was the average pay for one day's work.

Mary and Martha

Often Jesus told his disciples and the people around them not to become too caught up in what was going on around them. Money, good clothes, toys, and big houses were not as important as obeying God and learning all that Jesus had to say.

He told them, "Get the treasure in heaven that never runs out. Thieves can't steal it in heaven, and moths can't destroy it. Your heart will be where your treasure is."

He meant that if you always put God first in your mind, then your heart will tell you the right things to do. He taught this often, sometimes even to his closest friends.

For example, when the Lord and his disciples were traveling along, they came to the village of Bethany. There he stayed with some friends.

167

Martha, her sister Mary, and their brother Lazarus were all good friends to Jesus and were very special to him.

While Jesus was visiting, Mary sat down at Jesus' feet and listened to everything that Jesus said.

Martha, like her sister, was very excited that Jesus was visiting, but she knew how important it was to make sure that Jesus and all his disciples were comfortable and well fed. Martha was one of those special women who have a gift for making people feel loved and welcomed in her home. She enjoyed having Jesus and his disciples in her home, and she  worked hard to make sure they had all they needed. She wanted everything to be just right.

Martha became angry because she had so much work to do. The house needed to be cleaned, and food had to be prepared. Martha was a good hostess, but she would have liked to have had some help.

Martha was unhappy because her sister Mary continued to sit and listen to Jesus without helping her with any of the housework.

She went in and said, "Lord, don't you care that my sister has left me alone to do all the work? Tell her to help me!"

But the Lord answered her, "Martha, Martha, you are getting worried and upset about too many things. Only one thing is important. Mary has chosen the right thing, and it will never be taken away from her."

Martha understood. She relaxed and smiled. Although her duties were very important, she learned that the most important thing was to hear Jesus' words.

from **Luke 10:38–42; 12:33, 34**

Being Lost

A ll kinds of people who had sinned were crowded around Jesus, including tax collectors, who were considered some of the worst sinners.

The officials and others who held high places in the temple began to whisper about Jesus being friendly to these sinners. He even ate with them!

At that time the followers came to Jesus and asked, "Who is greatest in the kingdom of heaven?"

Jesus called a little child to him. He stood the child before the followers. Then he said, "I tell you the truth. You must change and become like little children. If you don't do this, you will never enter the kingdom of heaven. The greatest person in the kingdom of heaven is the one who makes himself humble like this child.

"Whoever accepts a little child in my name accepts me.

"Be careful. Don't think these little children are worth   *171* nothing. I tell you that they have angels in heaven who are always with my Father in heaven."

Then Jesus told them this story: "Suppose one of you has 100 sheep, but he loses 1 of them. Then he will leave the other 99 sheep alone and go out and look for the lost sheep. The man will keep on searching for the lost sheep until he finds it. And when he finds it, the man is very happy. He puts it on his shoulders and goes

home. He calls to his friends and neighbors and says, 'Be happy with me because I found my lost sheep!' In the same way, I tell you there is much joy in heaven when 1 sinner changes his heart. There is more joy for that 1 sinner than there is for 99 good people who don't need to change.

"Suppose a woman has ten silver coins,[n] but she loses one of them. She will light a lamp and clean the house. She will look carefully for the coin until she finds it. And when she finds it, she will call her friends and neighbors and say, 'Be happy with me because I have found the coin that I lost!' In the same way, there is joy before the angels of God when 1 sinner changes his heart."

from Matthew 18:1-5, 10; Luke 15:1-10

ⁿsilver coins A Roman denarius. One coin was the average pay for one day's work.

Raising Lazarus

There was a man named Lazarus who was sick. He lived in the town of Bethany. Lazarus was the brother of Mary and Martha, and all three of them were good friends of Jesus. So Mary and Martha sent someone to tell Jesus, "Lord, the one you love is sick."

174   When Jesus heard this he said, "This sickness will not end

in death. It is for the glory of God." Jesus loved Martha and her sister and Lazarus. But when he heard that Lazarus was sick, he stayed where he was for two more days. Then Jesus said to his followers, "Let us go back to Judea."

After Jesus said this, he added, "Our friend Lazarus has fallen asleep. But I am going there to wake him."

The followers said, "But Lord, if he can sleep, he will get well."

So then Jesus said plainly, "Lazarus is dead. And I am glad   *175* for your sakes that I was not there so that you may believe. But let us go to him now."

Jesus arrived in Bethany. There he learned that Lazarus had already been dead and in the tomb for four days. Bethany was about two miles from Jerusalem. Many Jews had come there to comfort Martha and Mary about their brother.

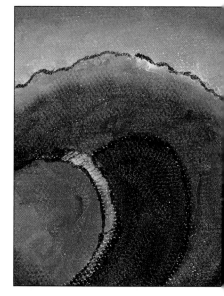

Martha heard that Jesus was coming, and she went out to meet him. But Mary stayed at home. Martha said to Jesus, "Lord, if you had been here, my brother would not have died. But I know that even now God will give you anything you ask."

Jesus said, "Your brother will rise and live again."

Martha answered, "I know that he will rise and live again in the resurrection[n] on the last day."

Jesus said to her, "I am the resurrection and the life. He who believes in me will have life even if he dies. And he who lives and believes in me will never die. Martha, do you believe this?"

Martha answered, "Yes, Lord."

Mary, too, went to see Jesus. The Jews were with Mary in the house, comforting her. They saw Mary stand and leave quickly. They followed her, thinking that she was going to the tomb to cry there.

Jesus saw that Mary was crying and that the Jews who came with her were crying, too. Jesus felt very sad in his heart and was deeply troubled. He asked, "Where did you bury him?"

"Come and see, Lord," they said.

Jesus cried.

So the Jews said, "See how much he loved him."

But some of them said, "If Jesus healed the eyes of the blind man, why didn't he keep Lazarus from dying?"

Again Jesus felt very sad in his heart. He came to the tomb. The tomb was a cave with a large stone covering the entrance. Jesus said, "Move the stone away."

Martha said, "But, Lord, it has been four days since he died. There will be a bad smell."

Then Jesus said to her, "Didn't I tell you that if you believed, you would see the glory of God?"

So they moved the stone away from the entrance. Then Jesus looked up and said, "Father, I thank you that you heard me. I know that you always hear me. But I said these things because of the people here around me. I want them to believe that you sent me." After Jesus said this, he cried out in a loud voice, "Lazarus, come out!" The dead man came out. His hands and feet were wrapped with pieces of cloth, and he had a cloth around his face.

Jesus said to them, "Take the cloth off of him and let him go."

There were many Jews who had come to visit Mary. They saw what Jesus did. And many of them believed in him.

from John 11:1–7, 11–15, 17–27, 31, 33–45

[n]resurrection Being raised from death to live again.

A Rich Fool

Jesus often told his disciples and the others around him that people who love and follow God should not spend time thinking about money or other things they think they need. God will make sure we have everything we need.

After all, God provides food for even the smallest of ani-

mals. If he cares about a small bird like a sparrow, then think how much more he cares for his children—those who love him.

Jesus said to his disciples: "So I tell you, don't worry about the food you need to live. Don't worry about the clothes you need for your body. Life is more important than clothes. Look at the birds. They don't plant or harvest. They don't save food in houses or barns. But God takes care of them. And you are worth much more than birds. None of you can add any time to your life by worrying about it. If you cannot do even the little things, then why worry about the big things? Look at the wild flowers. See how they grow. They don't work or make clothes for themselves. But I tell you that even Solomon, the great and rich king, was not dressed as beautifully as one of these flow-

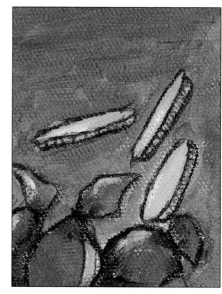

ers. God clothes the grass in the field like that. That grass is living today, but tomorrow it will be thrown into the fire. So you know how much more God will clothe you. Don't have so little faith! Don't always think about what you will eat or what you will drink. Don't worry about it. All the people in the world are trying to get these things. Your Father knows that you need them. The thing you should seek is God's kingdom. Then all the other things you need will be given to you.

Jesus was teaching a crowd when a man said to him, "Teacher, tell my brother to divide with me the property our father left us."

But Jesus said to him, "Who said that I should be your judge or decide how to divide the property between you two?" Then Jesus said to them, "Be careful and guard against all kinds of greed. A man's life is not measured by the many things he owns."

Then Jesus used this story: "There was a rich man who had some land, which grew a good crop of food. The rich man thought to himself, 'What will I do? I have no place to keep all my crops.' Then he said, 'I know what I will do. I will tear down my barns and build bigger ones! I will put all my grain and other goods together in my new barns. Then I can say to myself, I have enough good things stored to last for many years. Rest, eat, drink, and enjoy life!'

"But God said to that man, 'Foolish man! Tonight you will die. So who will get those things you have prepared for yourself?'"

Jesus told the crowd, "This is how it will be for anyone who stores things up only for himself and is not rich toward God."

from **Luke 12:13–31**

Zacchaeus

Jesus was going through the city of Jericho. In Jericho there was a man named Zacchaeus. He was a wealthy, very important tax collector.

Tax collectors then were not like tax collectors today. In Jesus' time, tax collectors were people who paid for the right to

collect taxes. They often made money by cheating people. They charged them too much and kept what they didn't have to pay to the government.

Most people hated tax collectors. They thought of them as traitors to their country and to their religion. They were thought of as sinners. But this sinner was determined to see Jesus and to hear what he was teaching.

He wanted to see who Jesus was, but he was too short to   *183* see above the crowd. He ran ahead to a place where he knew Jesus would come. He climbed a sycamore tree so he could see Jesus. When Jesus came to that place, he looked up and saw Zacchaeus in the tree. He said to him, "Zacchaeus, hurry and come down! I must stay at your house today."

Zacchaeus came down quickly. He was pleased to have Jesus in his house. All the people saw this and began to complain, "Look at the kind of man Jesus stays with. Zacchaeus is a sinner!"

But Zacchaeus said to the Lord, "I will give half of my money to the poor. If I have cheated anyone, I will pay that person back four times more!"

This was amazing! No one had ever heard of a tax collector paying back money, much less four times as much. This was a sign that Zacchaeus was truly sorry for all he had done wrong.

Jesus said to Zacchaeus, "Salvation has come to this house today. This man truly belongs to the family of Abraham. The Son of Man came to find lost people and save them."

As a tax collector who had cheated people, Zacchaeus had probably gotten very rich, but he was lost from God. But when he came to know Jesus, he became a new man. When he believed in Jesus as the Son of God, and when he believed what Jesus had taught him, he grew close to God again.

But Zacchaeus knew that real faith is not only believing and loving Jesus. It means that he had to turn from his old way of doing things—cheating and lying—and obey all God's commands. Real faith acts to make things right again.

from **Luke 19:1–9**

The Prodigal Son

Jesus told this story to a crowd of people:

"A man had two sons. The younger son said to his father, 'Give me my share of the property.' So the father divided the property between his two sons. Then the younger son gathered up all that was his and left. He traveled far away to another country. There he wasted his money in foolish living. He spent everything

that he had. Soon after that, the land became very dry, and there was no rain. There was not enough food to eat anywhere in the country. The son was hungry and needed money. So he got a job with one of the citizens there. The man sent the son into the fields to feed pigs. This was a terrible job, and he was still hungry. The son was so hungry that he was willing to eat the food the pigs were eating. But no one gave him anything. The son realized that he had been very foolish. He thought, 'All of my father's servants have plenty of food. But I am here, almost dying with hunger. I will leave and return to my father. I'll say to him: Father, I have sinned against God and have done wrong to you. I am not good enough to be called your son. But let me be like one of your servants.' So the son left and went to his father.

"While the son was still a long way off, his father saw him coming. He felt sorry for his son. So the father ran to him, and hugged and kissed him. The son said, 'Father, I have sinned against God and have done wrong to you. I am not good enough to be called your son.' But the father said to his servants, 'Hurry! Bring the best clothes and put them on him.

Also, put a ring on his finger and sandals on his feet. And get our fat calf and kill it. Then we can have a feast and celebrate! My son was dead, but now he is alive again! He was lost, but now he is found!' So they began to celebrate.

"The older son was in the field. As he came closer to the house, he heard the sound of music and dancing. So he called to one of the servants and asked, 'What does all this mean?' The servant said, 'Your brother has come back. Your father killed the fat calf to eat because your brother came home safely!' The older son was angry and would not go in to the feast. So the father went out and begged him to come in. The son said to his father, 'I have served you like a slave for many years! I have always obeyed your commands. But you never even killed a young goat for me to have a feast with my friends. But your other son has wasted all your money on foolish things. Then he comes home, and you kill the fat calf for him!' The father said to him, 'Son, you are always with me. All that I have is yours. We had to celebrate and be happy because your brother was dead, but now he is alive. He was lost, but now he is found.'"

In this way, Jesus reminds us that God always loves us, even when we disobey him and try to run away from him. He continues to care for us, and when we return to him, he celebrates.

from Luke 15:11–32

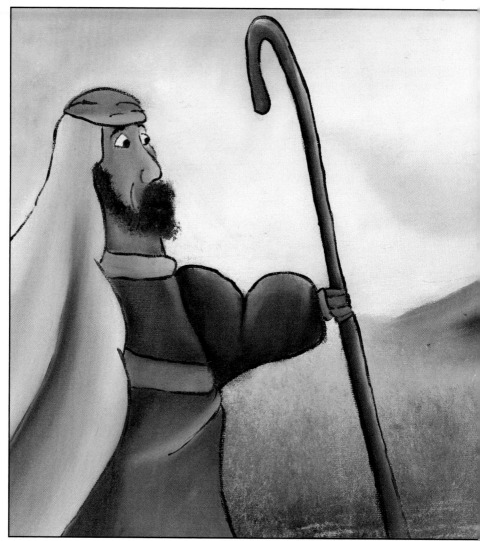

The Good Shepherd

J esus said:

"I am the good shepherd. The good shepherd gives his life for the sheep. The worker who is paid to keep the sheep is different from the shepherd who owns them. So when the worker sees a

wolf coming, he runs away and leaves the sheep alone. Then the

wolf attacks the sheep and scatters them. The man runs away because he is only a paid worker. He does not really care for the sheep.

"I am the good shepherd. I know my sheep, as the Father knows me. And my sheep know me, as I know the Father. I give my life for the sheep. I have other sheep that are not in this flock here. I must bring them also. They will listen to my voice, and there will be one flock and one shepherd."

We must remember that God takes care of us, no matter what. This has always been true. The great king David knew this when he wrote:

"The Lord is my shepherd.
I have everything I need.
He gives me rest in green
    pastures.
He leads me to calm water.
He gives me new strength.
For the good of his name,
    he leads me on paths
    that are right.
Even if I walk through a
    very dark valley,
I will not be afraid, because
    you are with me.
Your rod and your walking stick[n] comfort me.
You prepare a meal for me in front of my enemies.
You pour oil on my head.[n]
You give me more than I can hold.
Surely your goodness and love will be with me all my life.
And I will live in the house of the Lord forever."

***from* Psalm 23; John 10:11–16**

ⁿwalking stick The stick a shepherd uses to guide and protect his sheep.
ⁿpour oil . . . head This can mean that God gave him great wealth and blessed him.

The Triumphant Entry

Jesus and his followers were coming closer to Jerusalem. But first they stopped at Bethphage at the hill called the Mount of Olives. From there Jesus sent two of his followers into the town. He said to them, "Go to the town you can see there. When you enter it, you will find a donkey tied there with its colt. Untie them

and bring them to me. If anyone asks you why you are taking the donkeys, tell him, 'The Master needs them. He will send them back soon.'"

This was to make clear the full meaning of what the prophet said: "Tell the people of Jerusalem, 'Your king is coming to you. He is gentle and riding on a donkey. He is on the colt of a donkey.'"

They brought the donkey and the colt to Jesus. They laid   **195** their coats on the donkeys, and Jesus sat on them. Many people came to honor Jesus and to welcome him into Jerusalem. They spread their coats on the road before Jesus. Others cut branches from the trees and spread them on the road. Some of the people were walking ahead of Jesus. Others were walking behind him. All the people were shouting, "Praise[n] to the Son of David! God bless the One who comes in the name of the Lord! Praise to God in heaven!"

Then Jesus went into Jerusalem. The city was filled with excitement. The people asked, "Who is this man?"

The crowd answered, "This man is Jesus. He is the prophet from the town of Nazareth in Galilee."

Some of the Pharisees said to Jesus, "Teacher, tell your followers not to say these things!"

But Jesus answered, "I tell you, if my followers don't say these things, then the stones will cry out."

Jesus went into the Temple. He began to throw out the people who were selling things there. He said, "It is written in the Scriptures, 'My Temple will be a house where people will pray.'[n] But you have changed it into a 'hideout for robbers'!"[n]

Jesus taught in the Temple every day. The leading priests, the teachers of the law, and some of the leaders of the people wanted to kill Jesus. But all the people were listening closely to him and were interested in all the things he said. So the leading priests, the teachers of the law, and the leaders did not know how they could kill him.

from Matthew 21:1–5, 7–11; Luke 19:32–34, 39, 40, 45–48

[n]Praise Literally, "Hosanna," a Hebrew word used at first in praying to God for help. At this time it was probably a shout of joy used in praising God or his Messiah.
[n]"My Temple . . . pray.' Quotation from Isaiah 56:7.
[n]'hideout for robbers' Quotation from Jeremiah 7:11.

The Last Supper

On the first day of the Feast of Unleavened Bread, the followers came to Jesus. They said, "We will prepare everything for you to eat the Passover Feast. Where do you want to have the feast?"

Jesus answered, "Go into the city to a certain man. Tell him that the Teacher says, 'The chosen time is near. I will have the Passover Feast with my followers at your house.'" The followers

did what Jesus told them to do, and they prepared the Passover Feast.

In the evening Jesus was sitting at the table with his 12 followers. They were all eating. Then Jesus said, "I tell you the truth. One of you 12 will turn against me."

This made the followers very sad. Each one said to Jesus, "Surely, Lord, I am not the one who will turn against you. Am I?"

Jesus answered, "The man who has dipped his hand with me into the bowl is the one who will turn against me. The Son of

Man will die. The Scriptures say this will happen. But how terrible it will be for the person who gives the Son of Man to be killed. It would be better for him if he had never been born."

Then Judas said to Jesus, "Teacher, surely I am not the one. Am I?" (Judas is the one who would give Jesus to his enemies.)

Jesus answered, "Yes, it is you."

While they were eating, Jesus took some bread. He thanked God for it and broke it. Then he gave it to his followers and said, "Take this bread and eat it. This bread is my body."

Then Jesus took a cup. He thanked God for it and gave it to the followers. He said, "Every one of you drink this. This is my blood which begins the new agreement that God makes with his people. This blood is poured out for many to forgive their sins. I tell you this: I will not drink of this fruit of the vine[n] again until that day when I drink it new with you in my Father's kingdom."

They sang a hymn. Then they went out to the Mount of Olives.

Jesus told his followers, "Tonight you will lose your faith because of me. It is written in the Scriptures: 'I will kill the shepherd, and the sheep will scatter.'[n] But after I rise from death, I will go ahead of you into Galilee."

Peter said, "All the other followers may lose their faith because of you. But I will never lose my faith."

Jesus said, "I tell you the truth. Tonight you will say you

don't know me. You will say this three times before the rooster crows."

But Peter said, "I will never say that I don't know you! I will even die with you!" And all the other followers said the same thing.

from **Matthew 26:17–35**

<hr />

ⁿfruit of the vine Product of the grapevine; this may also be translated "wine."

ⁿ"I will . . . scatter.' Quotation from Zechariah 13:7.

The Garden of Gethsemane

Then Jesus went with his followers to a place called Gethsemane. He said to them, "Sit here while I go over there and pray." He told Peter and the two sons of Zebedee to come with him. Then Jesus began to be very sad and troubled.

He said to Peter and the two sons of Zebedee, "My heart is full of sorrow and breaking with sadness. Stay here with me and watch."

Then Jesus walked a little farther away from them. He fell to the ground and prayed, "My Father, if it is possible, do not give me this cup^n of suffering. Is there any other way I can go through this? But do what you want, not what I want." Then Jesus went back to his followers and found them asleep. Jesus said to Peter, "You men could not stay awake with me for one hour? Stay awake

203

and pray for strength against temptation. Your spirit wants to do what is right. But your body is weak."

Then Jesus went away a second time. He prayed, "My Father, if it is possible for this painful thing to be taken from me, and if I must do it, then I pray that what you want will be done."

Then Jesus went back to the followers. Again he found them asleep, because their eyes were heavy. So Jesus left them and went away one more time and prayed. The third time he prayed, he said the same thing.

God was not forcing Jesus to do anything. Although Jesus knew that what he was about to face would be difficult, he chose to do God's will all on his own. At that moment the Lord sent an angel from heaven to give Jesus the strength that he would need to get through this very difficult time.

Then Jesus went back to the followers and said, "You are still sleeping and resting? The time has come for the Son of Man to be given to the sinful people. Get up. We must go. Here comes the man who has turned against me."

While Jesus was still speaking, Judas came up. Judas was 1 of the 12 followers. He had many people with him. They had been sent from the leading priests and the older leaders of the people. They carried swords and clubs. Judas had planned to give them a signal. He had said, "The man I kiss is Jesus. Arrest him." At once Judas went to Jesus and said, "Greetings, Teacher!" Then Judas

kissed him.

Jesus answered, "Friend, do the thing you came to do."

Then the men came and grabbed Jesus and arrested him. When that happened, one of Jesus' followers reached for his sword and pulled it out. The follower struck the servant of the high priest with the sword and cut off his ear.

Jesus said to the man, "Put your sword back in its place. All who use swords will be killed with swords. Surely you know I could ask my Father, and he would give me more than 12 armies of angels. But this thing must happen this way so that it will be as the Scriptures say."

Then Jesus said to the crowd, "You came to get me with swords and clubs as if I were a criminal. Every day I sat in the Temple teaching. You did not arrest me there. But all these things have happened so that it will be as the prophets wrote." Then all of Jesus' followers left him and ran away.

from Matthew 26:36–56

[n]cup Jesus is talking about the bad things that will happen to him. Accepting these things will be very hard, like drinking a cup of something that tastes very bitter.

The Road to the Cross

After his arrest, Jesus was brought before Pilate, who was the governor. The people who had brought Jesus began to accuse him. They told Pilate, "We caught this man telling things that were confusing our people. He says that we should not pay taxes to Caesar. He calls himself the Christ, a king."

Pilate asked Jesus, "Are you the king of the Jews?"

Jesus answered, "Yes, that is right."

Pilate said to the leading priests and the people, "I find nothing wrong with this man."

He said to them, "You brought this man to me. You said that he was making trouble among the people. But I have questioned him before you all, and I have not found him guilty of the things you say. . . . Look, he has done nothing for which he should die. So, after I punish him, I will let him go free."

But all the people shouted, "Kill him!"

Pilate asked them, "Do you want me to free the king of the Jews?" Pilate knew that the leading priests had given Jesus to him because they were jealous of Jesus. Pilate obviously thought Jesus was innocent. Because there was a tradition of releasing one prisoner during Passover, Pilate was offering the people who were accusing Jesus a way to let him go without losing their honor.

But they shouted again, "Kill him! Kill him on a cross!"

A third time Pilate said to them, "Why? What wrong has he done? I can find no reason to kill him. So I will have him punished and set him free."

But they continued to shout. They demanded that Jesus be killed on the cross. Their yelling became so loud that Pilate decided to give them what they wanted.

The soldiers led Jesus away. At that time, there was a man coming into the city from the fields. His name was Simon, and he was from the city of Cyrene which is in northern Africa. The soldiers forced Simon to carry Jesus' cross and walk behind him. Because Jesus had been beaten, he was no longer able to carry the cross.

A large crowd of people was following Jesus. Some of the women were sad and crying. But Jesus turned and said to them, "Women of Jerusalem, don't cry for me. Cry for yourselves and for your children too!"

from Mark 15:9, 10; Luke 23:1–4, 14–18a, 20–28

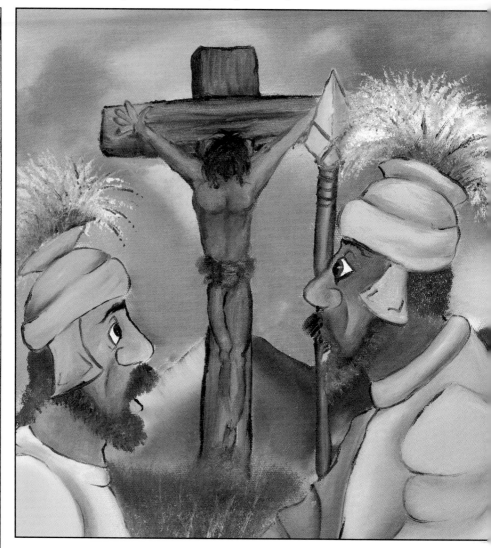

The Crucifixion

A fter Jesus had been brought before Pilate and beaten, soldiers took him to Golgotha. (Golgotha means the Place of the Skull.) At Golgotha the soldiers tried to give Jesus wine to drink. This wine was mixed with myrrh. But he refused to drink it. The soldiers nailed Jesus to a cross. Then they divided his clothes

among themselves. They threw lots to decide which clothes each soldier would get.

It was nine o'clock in the morning when they nailed Jesus to the cross. There was a sign with the charge against Jesus written on it. The sign read: "THE KING OF THE JEWS." They also put two robbers on crosses beside Jesus, one on the right, and the other on the left.

Jesus said, "Father, forgive them. They don't know what they are doing."[n]

The people stood there watching. The leaders made fun of Jesus. They said, "If he is God's Chosen One, the Christ, then let him save himself. He saved other people, didn't he?"

One of the criminals began to shout insults at Jesus: "Aren't you the Christ? Then save yourself! And save us too!"

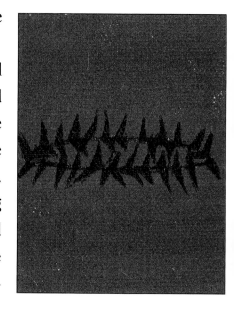

But the other criminal stopped him. He said, "You should fear God! You are getting the same punishment he is. We are punished justly; we should die. But this man has done nothing wrong!" Then this criminal said to Jesus, "Jesus, remember me when you come into your kingdom!"

Then Jesus said to him, "Listen! What I say is true: Today you will be with me in paradise!"[n]

It was about noon, and the whole land became dark until three o'clock in the afternoon. There was no sun! . . . Jesus cried out in a loud voice, "Father, I give you my life." After Jesus said this, he died.

Some women were standing at a distance from the cross, watching. Some of these women were Mary Magdalene, Salome, and Mary the mother of James and Joseph. (James was her youngest son.) These were the women who followed Jesus in Galilee and cared for him.

This was Preparation Day. (That means the day before the Sabbath day.) It was becoming dark. A man named Joseph from Arimathea was brave enough to go to Pilate and ask for Jesus' body. Joseph was an important member of the Jewish council. He was one of the people who wanted the kingdom of God to come. Pilate wondered if Jesus was already dead. Pilate called the army officer who guarded Jesus and asked him if Jesus had already died. The officer told Pilate that he was dead. So Pilate told Joseph he could have the body. Joseph bought some linen cloth, took the body down from the cross and wrapped it in the linen. He put the body in a tomb that was cut in a wall of rock. Then he closed the tomb by rolling a very large stone to cover the entrance. And Mary Magdalene and Mary the mother of Joseph saw the place where Jesus was laid.

from Mark 15:22–30, 40–47; Luke 23:34, 35, 39–46, 49

[n]Verse 34 Some early Greek copies do not have this part of the verse.
[n]paradise A place where good people go when they die.

The Resurrection

The day after the Sabbath day was the first day of the week. At dawn on the first day, Mary Magdalene and another woman named Mary went to look at the tomb.

At that time there was a strong earthquake. An angel of the Lord came down from heaven. The angel went to the tomb and

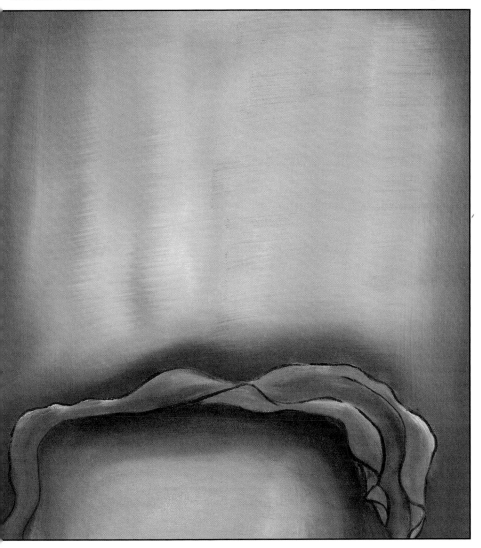

rolled the stone away from the entrance. Then he sat on the stone. He was shining as bright as lightning. His clothes were white as snow. The soldiers guarding the tomb were very frightened of the angel. They shook with fear and then became like dead men.

The angel said to the women, "Don't be afraid. I know that you are looking for Jesus, the one who was killed on the cross. But he is not here. He has risen from death as he said he would. Come and see the place where his body was. And go quickly and tell his followers. Say to them: 'Jesus has risen from death. He is going

into Galilee. He will be there before you. You will see him there.'"
Then the angel said, "Now I have told you."

The women left the tomb quickly. They were afraid, but
they were also very happy. They ran to tell Jesus' followers what

had happened. Suddenly, Jesus
met them and said, "Greetings."
The women came up to Jesus,
took hold of his feet, and worshiped him. Then Jesus said to
them, "Don't be afraid. Go and tell
my brothers to go on to Galilee.
They will see me there."

The women went to tell Jesus' followers. At the same time,
some of the soldiers who had been
guarding the tomb went into the city. They went to tell the leading priests everything that had happened. Then the priests met
with the older Jewish leaders and made a plan. They paid the soldiers a large amount of money. They said to the soldiers, "Tell the
people that Jesus' followers came during the night and stole the
body while you were asleep. If the governor hears about this, we
will satisfy him and save you from trouble." So the soldiers kept
the money and obeyed the priests. And that story is still spread
among the Jews even today.

The 11 followers went to Galilee. They went to the mountain where Jesus told them to go. On the mountain they saw Jesus
and worshiped him. But some of them did not believe that it was
really Jesus. Then Jesus came to them and said, "All power in
heaven and on earth is given to me. So go and make followers of
all people in the world. Baptize them in the name of the Father

and the Son and the Holy Spirit. Teach them to obey everything that I have told you. You can be sure that I will be with you always. I will continue with you until the end of the world."

After the Lord Jesus said these things to the followers, he was carried up into heaven. There, Jesus sat at the right side of God.

from **Matthew 28:1–20; Mark 16:19**

On the Road to Emmaus

On the road to Emmaus, two of Jesus' disciples were talking and thinking about the reports that Jesus had been seen after he was crucified and buried. Just then, Jesus approached and began walking alongside of them, but they did not recognize him.

Then he said, "What are these things you are talking about while you walk?"

The two followers stopped. Their faces were very sad. The one named Cleopas answered, "You must be the only one in Jerusalem who does not know what just happened there."

Jesus said to them, "What are you talking about?"

The followers said, "It is about Jesus of Nazareth. He was a prophet from God to all the people. He said and did many powerful things. Our leaders and priests gave him up to be judged and killed. They nailed him to a cross. But we were hoping that he would free the Jews. It is now the third day since this happened. And today some women among us told us some amazing things.

Early this morning they went to the tomb, but they did not find his body there. They came and told us that they had seen a vision of angels. The angels said that Jesus was alive! So some of our group went to the tomb, too. They found it just as the women said, but they did not see Jesus."

Then Jesus said to them, "You are foolish and slow to realize what is true. You should believe everything the prophets said. They said that the Christ must suffer these things before he enters his glory." Then Jesus began to explain everything that had been written about himself in the Scriptures. He started with Moses, and then he talked about what all the prophets had said about him.

They came near the town of Emmaus, and Jesus acted as if he did not plan to stop there. But they begged him, "Stay with us. It is late; it is almost night." So he went in to stay with them.

Jesus sat down with them and took some bread. He gave thanks for the food and divided it. Then he gave it to them. And then, they were allowed to recognize Jesus. But when they saw who he was, he disappeared. They said to each other, "When Jesus talked to us on the road, it felt like a fire burning in us. It was exciting when he explained the true meaning of the Scriptures."

So the two followers got up at once and went back to Jerusalem. There they found the 11 apostles and others gathered. They were saying, "The Lord really has risen from death! He showed himself to Simon."

Then the two followers told what had happened on the road. They talked about how they recognized Jesus when he divided the bread.

from **Luke 24:13–35**

Doubting Thomas

On the same day that he appeared to Mary outside his tomb, Jesus appeared that evening to all the disciples. The doors were locked, because they were afraid of the Jews. Then Jesus came and stood among them. He said, "Peace be with you!" After he said this, he showed them his hands and his side—his wounds

from being nailed to the cross. The followers were very happy when they saw the Lord.

Then Jesus said again, "Peace be with you! As the Father sent me, I now send you." After he said this, he breathed on them and said, "Receive the Holy Spirit. If you forgive anyone his sins, they are forgiven. If you don't forgive them, they are not forgiven."

Thomas (called Didymus) was not with the followers when   **223**

Jesus came. Thomas was 1 of the 12. The other followers told Thomas, "We saw the Lord."

But Thomas refused to believe. He said, "I will not believe it until I see the nail marks in his hands. And I will not believe until I put my finger where the nails were and put my hand into his side."

A week later the followers were in the house again. Thomas was with them. The doors were locked, but Jesus came in and stood among them. He said, "Peace be with you!" Then he said to Thomas, "Put your hand here in my side. Stop doubting and believe."

Thomas said to him, "My Lord and my God!"

Then Jesus told him, "You believe because you see me. Those who believe without seeing me will be truly happy."

Later, Jesus showed himself to his followers by Lake Galilee.[n] This is how it happened: Some of the followers were together. They were Simon Peter, Thomas (called Didymus), Nathanael from Cana in Galilee, the two sons of Zebedee, and two other followers. Simon Peter said, "I am going out to fish."

The other followers said, "We will go with you." So they went out and got into the boat. They fished that night but caught nothing.

Early the next morning Jesus stood on the shore. But the followers did not know that it was Jesus. Then he said to them,

"Friends, have you caught any fish?"

They answered, "No."

He said, "Throw your net into the water on the right side of the boat, and you will find some." So they did this. They caught so many fish that they could not pull the net back into the boat.

When the followers stepped out of the boat and onto the shore, they saw a fire of hot coals. There were fish on the fire, and there was bread.

Then Jesus said, "Bring some of the fish that you caught."

Jesus said to them, "Come and eat." None of the followers dared ask him, "Who are you?" They knew it was the Lord. Jesus came and took the bread and gave it to them. He also gave them the fish.

This was now the third time Jesus showed himself to his followers after he was raised from death.

Jesus did many other miracles before his followers that are not written in this book. The miracles that are recorded in the Bible are so that you can believe that Jesus is the Christ, the Son of God. Then, by believing, you can have life through his name.

from **John 20:19–31; 21:1–6, 9, 10, 12–14**

[n]Lake Galilee Literally, "Sea of Tiberias."

Peter and John on Trial

After Jesus came and spoke to the disciples and filled them with the Holy Spirit, the disciples went out and performed miracles in the name of Jesus. Peter and John healed a man who could not walk. Teaching the people God's law angered the priests

and other officials. So they had Peter and John arrested. Already a lot of people had heard the disciples' message and believed it.

The next day the Jewish leaders, the older Jewish leaders, and the teachers of the law met in Jerusalem. They made Peter and John stand before them. The Jewish leaders asked them: "By what power or authority did you do this?"

Then Peter was filled with the Holy Spirit. He said to them, "Rulers of the people, are you questioning us about a good thing that was done to a crippled man? Are you asking us who made him well? We want all of you and all the Jewish people to know that the man was made well by the power of Jesus Christ from Nazareth! You nailed him to a cross, but God raised him from death. This man was crippled, but he is now well and able to stand

here before you because of the power of Jesus! Jesus is the only One who can save people. His name is the only power in the world that has been given to save people. And we must be saved through him!"

The Jewish leaders saw that Peter and John were not afraid to speak. They understood that these men had no special training or education. So they were amazed. Then they realized that Peter and John had been with Jesus. They saw the crippled man standing there beside the two apostles. They saw that the man was healed. So they could say nothing against them. The Jewish leaders told them to leave the meeting. Then the leaders talked to each other about what they should do. They said, "What shall we do with these men? Everyone in Jerusalem knows that they have done a great miracle! We cannot say it is not true. But we must warn them not to talk to people anymore using that name. Then this thing will not spread among the people."

So they called Peter and John in again. They told them not to speak or to teach at all in the name of Jesus. But Peter and John answered them, "What do you think is right? What would God want? Should we obey you or God? We cannot keep quiet. We must speak about what we have seen and heard." The Jewish leaders could not find a way to punish them because all the people were praising God for what had been done. (This miracle was a proof from God. The man who was healed was more than 40 years old!) So the Jewish leaders warned the apostles again and let them go free.

from **Acts 4:5, 7–10, 12–22**

Saul on the Road to Damascus

There were many who hated Jesus. Saul was an evil man who especially hated Jesus and all his followers. People began trying to hurt the church in Jerusalem and make it suffer. Saul was also trying to destroy the church. He went from house to house.

He dragged out men and women and put them in jail. All the believers, except the apostles, went to different places in Judea and Samaria. And everywhere they were scattered, they told people the Good News.

In Jerusalem Saul was still trying to frighten the followers of the Lord by saying he would kill them. So he went to the high priest and asked him to write letters to the synagogues in the city of Damascus. Saul wanted the high priest to give him the authority to find people in Damascus who were followers of Christ's Way.

231

If he found any there, men or women, he would arrest them and bring them back to Jerusalem.

So Saul went to Damascus. As he came near the city, a bright light from heaven suddenly flashed around him. Saul fell to the ground. He heard a voice saying to him, "Saul, Saul! Why are you doing things against me?"

Saul said, "Who are you, Lord?"

The voice answered, "I am Jesus. I am the One you are trying to hurt. Get up now and go into the city. Someone there will tell you what you must do."

The men traveling with Saul stood there, but they said nothing. They heard the voice, but they saw no one. Saul got up from the ground. He opened his eyes, but he could not see. So the men with Saul took his hand and led him into Damascus. For three days Saul could not see, and he did not eat or drink.

There was a follower of Jesus in Damascus named Ananias. The Lord spoke to Ananias in a vision, "Ananias!"

Ananias answered, "Here I am, Lord."

The Lord said to him, "Get up and go to the street called Straight Street. Find the house of Judas.^{n} Ask for a man named Saul from the city of Tarsus. He is there now, praying. Saul has seen a vision. In it a man named Ananias comes to him and lays his hands on him. Then he sees again."

But Ananias answered, "Lord, many people have told me about this man and the terrible things he did to your people in

Jerusalem. Now he has come here to Damascus. The leading priests have given him the power to arrest everyone who worships you."

But the Lord said to Ananias, "Go! I have chosen Saul for an important work. He must tell about me to non-Jews, to kings, and to the people of Israel. I will show him how much he must suffer for my name."

So Ananias went to the house of Judas. He laid his hands on Saul and said, "Brother Saul, the Lord Jesus sent me. He is the one you saw on the road on your way here. He sent me so that you can see again and be filled with the Holy Spirit." Immediately, something that looked like fish scales fell from Saul's eyes. He was able to see again! Then Saul got up and was baptized. After eating some food, his strength returned.

Saul stayed with the followers of Jesus in Damascus for a few days. Soon he began to preach about Jesus in the synagogues, saying, "Jesus is the Son of God!"

All the people who heard him were amazed because they remembered the old Saul. Saul became a great speaker for the Lord.

from **Acts 8:1–3; 9:1–22**

[n]Judas This is not either of the apostles named Judas.

Philip
and the Ethiopian

Jerusalem had been the main place that the gospel was preached, until the Lord's followers were run out of town by the enemies of Jesus. Perhaps they thought they would stop the spread of the gospel, but this was not the case. In fact, the oppo-

site happened and fulfilled what Jesus said his followers should do: Take the gospel to all nations.

Philip[n] went to the city of Samaria and preached about the Christ. The people there heard Philip and saw the miracles he was doing. They all listened carefully to the things he said. Many of these people had evil spirits in them. But Philip made the evil spirits leave them. The spirits made a loud noise when they came out. There were also many weak and crippled people there. Philip healed them, too. So the people in that city were very happy.

235

After Philip had been in Samaria for some time, an angel of the Lord spoke to Philip. The angel said, "Get ready and go south. Go to the road that leads down to Gaza from Jerusalem—the desert road." So Philip got ready and left. On the road he saw a

man from Ethiopia, a eunuch. He was an important officer in the service of Candace, the queen of the Ethiopians. He was responsible for taking care of all her money. He had gone to Jerusalem to worship, and now he was sitting in his chariot and reading from the book of Isaiah, the prophet. The Spirit said to Philip, "Go to that chariot and stay near it."

So Philip ran toward the chariot. He heard the man reading from Isaiah, the prophet. Philip asked, "Do you understand what you are reading?"

He answered, "How can I understand? I need someone to explain it to me!" Then he invited Philip to climb in and sit with him.

The officer said to Philip, "Please tell me, who is the prophet talking about? Is he talking about himself or about someone else?" Philip began to speak. He started with this same Scripture and told the man the Good News about Jesus.

While they were traveling down the road, they came to some water. The officer said, "Look! Here is water! What is stopping me from being baptized?" Then the officer commanded the chariot to stop. Both Philip and the officer went down into the water, and Philip baptized him. When they came up out of the water, the Spirit of the Lord took Philip away; the officer never saw him again. The officer continued on his way home, full of joy.

from **Acts 8:5–8, 25–31, 34–39**

*ⁿ*Philip Not the apostle named Philip.

Paul's Journeys

J esus commanded his disciples, "You will be my witnesses—in Jerusalem, in all of Judea, in Samaria, and in every part of the world." He wanted everyone to hear the message of salvation. Paul was a disciple of Jesus Christ and spread the gospel to many people who were outside the Jewish faith.

Paul made three journeys to spread the good news of Jesus

Christ. On one of the trips, Paul and Silas were thrown into jail for sending an evil spirit out of a slave girl.

About midnight Paul and Silas were praying and singing songs to God. The other prisoners were listening to them. Suddenly, there was a big earthquake. It was so strong that it shook the foundation of the jail. Then all the doors of the jail broke open. All the prisoners were freed from their chains. The jailer woke up and saw that the jail doors were open. He thought that the prisoners had already escaped. So he got his sword and was

239

about to kill himself.[n] But Paul shouted, "Don't hurt yourself! We are all here!"

The jailer told someone to bring a light. Then he ran inside. Shaking with fear, he fell down before Paul and Silas. Then he brought them outside and said, "Men, what must I do to be saved?"

They said to him, "Believe in the Lord Jesus and you will be saved—you and all the people in your house."

On another trip, Paul was again a prisoner being transported by boat to Rome to be tried by the emperor. On the way, the ship was caught in a terrible storm. The next day the storm was blowing them so hard that the men threw out some of the cargo, trying to keep the ship from sinking. For many days they could not see the sun or the stars. The storm was very bad. They lost all hope of staying alive—they thought they would die.

But Paul stood up before the men and said, "This is the God I worship. I am his. God will save the lives of the men sailing with me. Everything will happen as his angel told me. But we will crash on an island."

For fourteen days and nights, the ship was blown around. Finally, the ship's crew saw a coast with a beach. They ran the ship aground. The captain ordered everyone who could swim to jump into the water and swim to land. The rest used wooden boards or pieces of the ship. And this is how all the people made it safely to land.

This island was called Malta, and the people who lived there welcomed the crew. Paul healed the father of the governor. After this, all the other sick people on the island came to Paul, and he healed them, too. The people on the island gave Paul and his friends **many honors**. When they finally sailed, they gave them everything they needed.

from **Acts 1; 16; 27; 28**

[n]**kill himself** He thought the leaders would kill him for letting his prisoners escape.   *241*

Timothy

Timothy was one of the greatest students of the apostle Paul. Timothy was the son of a Greek father and a Jewish Christian mother, and he traveled many miles with Paul, who loved him as if he were Paul's own son.

When they were not traveling together, Paul often wrote to

his student Timothy to give him instructions on how to live and how to teach the good news about Jesus. Paul knew that he was not the only one who had taught Timothy: he had learned much about the Scriptures from his Christian mother and grandmother. Timothy had learned so much from them that he was truly ready for Paul's teaching. Timothy was the one responsible for strengthening the church in Macedonia, and Paul sent him on many missions to Thessalonica and Corinth.

Timothy was young, and Paul tried to guide and teach him to be a better servant of the Lord. Timothy was sensitive, devoted, and loyal, but he still suffered from temptations and fearfulness.

Paul's second letter to Timothy reminds us of how much Paul loved God and wanted to show Timothy and all of those who love Jesus how to live the way Jesus wants us to.

Paul wrote:

To Timothy, a dear son to me. Grace, mercy, and peace to you from God the Father and Christ Jesus our Lord.

I always remember you in my prayers, day and night. And I thank God for you in these prayers. He is the God my ancestors served. And I serve him, doing what I know is right. I remember that you cried for me. And I want very much to see you so that I can be filled with joy. I remember your true faith. That kind of faith first belonged to your grandmother Lois and to your mother Eunice. And I know that you now have that same faith. That is why I remind you to use the gift God gave you. God gave you that gift when I laid my hands on[n] you. Now let it grow, as a small flame grows into a fire. God did not give us a spirit that makes us afraid. He gave us a spirit of power and love and self-control.

So do not be ashamed to tell people about our Lord Jesus. . . . But suffer with me for the Good News. God gives us the

strength to do that.

Jesus destroyed death. And through the Good News, he showed us the way to have life that cannot be destroyed.

from 2 Timothy 1:2–8, 10

---

*n*laid . . . on A sign to show that Paul had power from God to give Timothy a special blessing.

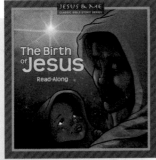
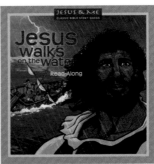

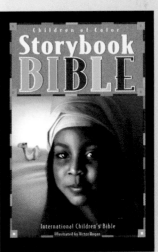